ST MARY'S
A SOCIAL HIST

CW00498398

*For the priests and people
of St Mary's R.C. Parish
Hamilton*

ST MARY'S HAMILTON

A SOCIAL HISTORY 1846–1996

edited by
Thomas M. Devine

JOHN DONALD PUBLISHERS LTD
EDINBURGH

ISBN 0 85976 429 X

The publisher acknowledges subsidy
from the Scottish Arts Council
towards the publication of this volume.

British Library Cataloguing in Publication Data
A catalogue record for this book is available from the
BritishLibrary.

Typeset by WestKey Ltd., Falmouth, Cornwall.
Printed and bound by Bell & Bain Ltd., Glasgow.

Preface

The principal purpose of this book is to help to celebrate the 150th anniversary in 1996 of the opening of St Mary's RC Church in Hamilton. Commemorative parish histories are not uncommon, but it is perhaps fair to say that this is one with a difference. Due attention is given to the specifically religious features of parish development but, in addition, the community of the parish is considered in detail. Education, political and social attitudes, sectarianism, and relations with the wider community are all examined. The result is a social history of Catholicism in one Scottish town over 150 years.

The book charts the development of a poor Irish immigrant community in the early nineteenth century, through many generations, to the last decade of the twentieth century, when their descendants have become fully integrated members of Scottish society. The first chapters focus on the establishment of the parish and the formation of a Catholic community with a clear identity by the early twentieth century. Most of the remaining chapters concentrate on the more recent past. Based on questionnaire evidence provided by parish members and other survey techniques, these sections provide new insights into modern Catholic attitudes towards key political and moral issues. The St Mary's parish of the 1990s contains significant numbers of well-educated professional families. In that sense it is not perhaps representative of the majority of Catholic parishes in Scotland. But many Catholics have moved into the middle classes over the last three decades, and this book is one of the first to survey their attitudes and values in depth.

The contributors therefore hope that the volume will have wide appeal, not only to the parishioners of St Mary's themselves, for whom it is primarily intended, but to all who are interested in the history of Scottish Catholicism and its current place in Scottish society

T. M. Devine

Acknowledgements

The help and assistance of the following, who supplied information and photographic material, and in other ways contributed to this project, are gratefully acknowledged: Angelina De Marco; Anne Marie Di Mambro; John Di Mambro; Audrey Drummond; Hamilton District Museum; Hamilton Public Library; Margaret Hastie; Walter Maxwell; E. Morgan; John McCaffrey; Agnes McCormick; Sheila McGuire; James McKenna; Andy McLaughlan; M. McVey; John Scanlon. Dr Bradley wishes to extend a special thanks to all those who responded so fully to his survey questionnaires and to the subsequent interviews.

This volume would not have been possible without the encouragement of Monsignor Alexander Devanney, VG, parish priest of St Mary's, Hamilton. The contributors are particularly grateful to him for supporting the idea of a Catholic parish history with a difference.

Contents

List of Illustrations

Notes on Contributors

Dr Joseph M. Bradley graduated with a Ph.D from Strathclyde University's Department of Government in 1993. His book, *Ethnic and Religious Identity in Modern Scotland: Culture, Politics and Football*, was published by Avebury in June 1995. He is currently a Research Fellow in the Social Sciences at Glasgow Caledonian University.

Professor Thomas M. Devine, FBA, is Professor of Scottish History, Director of the Research Centre in Scottish History, and Deputy Principal, University of Strathclyde. He is the author of numerous books and articles on Scottish historical studies and related issues.

Dr James Douglas is a deacon of St Mary's Parish and former Principal Teacher of History at Holy Cross High School, Hamilton.

Dr Mary McHugh obtained her doctorate from the University of Strathclyde on the history of the Catholic Church in Scotland from the later nineteenth century to the present. She is Archivist of the Archdiocese of Glasgow.

Martin J. Mitchell is a graduate in Modern History of the University of Strathclyde and is currently completing a Ph.D there in the Research Centre in Scottish History on Irish Immigrants and Scottish Politics and Society in the First Half of the Nineteenth Century.

CHAPTER 1

The Establishment and Early Years of the Hamilton Mission

Martin J. Mitchell

The Catholic Church in the West of Scotland c.1790–c.1850

It has been estimated that by the mid-1790s there were only 30,000 Roman Catholics in Scotland out of a population of around 1.5 million. One half of this number lived in the Highlands, mainly in the Morar region in the west, and on some of the Hebridean islands, such as South Uist, Barra, and Benbecula. Most of those who lived in the Lowlands resided in the north-east, particularly in Banffshire, although small groups of Catholics could be found in Perthshire, Dundee, and Edinburgh. Priests and chapels were present in these areas. Elsewhere, there were clergymen who served as chaplains to the Catholic landed families of Traquair in Peeblesshire, Terregles, in Dumfrieshire, and Munshes and Kirkconnell, in Kirkcudbrightshire. These priests were maintained by the lairds and said mass in their employers' private chapels, although the Scottish Catholic Church expected them to minister to any Catholic families in the surrounding districts. In the western Lowland counties – Lanarkshire, Dunbartonshire, Renfrewshire, Ayrshire, and Wigtownshire – there was only one chapel, at Glasgow, where the priest attended to a congregation of between five and six hundred. Most of this number were Highlanders who had recently migrated to find employment in the cotton factories in and around the city. Indeed, the placing of a priest in Glasgow and the establishment of the chapel, both in 1792, had been a result of this movement, which had begun the previous year.

Prior to these developments the Catholics of Glasgow, who numbered less than one hundred, had been accustomed, since

1781, to receiving regular visits from Bishop Geddes of Edinburgh. Initially he said mass in the house of one of the city's Catholics, but as numbers increased this proved to be inadequate, and in 1789 a larger apartment was rented for the congregation. Outside of Glasgow, not only were there no chapels in Lanarkshire and the other western Lowland counties in the mid-1790s; there were also not any priests stationed there. Before the second half of the 1780s there had been few or no Catholics in these areas and therefore no need for clergymen. During the next ten years small groups of Irish vagrants and workers began to appear in the region, particularly in the counties of Wigtownshire and Ayrshire. The Catholic Church was not, however, capable of providing priests for these immigrants.[1]

Forty years later, as a result of large-scale Irish immigration, this pattern of Scottish Catholicism had altered significantly. By the mid-1830s the number of Roman Catholics in the western lowland counties alone had risen to around 70,000 – almost all of them Irish or second (or even third) generation Irish immigrants.[2] Chapels were built in the region and priests settled there.[3] For example, in Glasgow, the chapel of 1792 had been replaced in 1797 by a larger one. As increasing numbers of Irish settled in and around the city this building soon proved to be too small. The priest at Glasgow, Andrew Scott, (who became a Bishop in 1828) decided to build a larger church on a different site, and towards the end of 1816 St Andrew's church, later the Cathedral, was opened in Great Clyde Street. A second smaller chapel, in the Gorbals, was opened in 1826. By late 1835 these two chapels were served by four priests, at a time when the congregation of the Glasgow Mission numbered around 50,000.[4]

Elsewhere, missions were founded only when priests became available and when there were enough Catholics settled in an area to support the clergyman and the mission. For example, in 1808 Ayr, Paisley, and Greenock were each sent a priest. Once settled in these towns the clergymen hired halls in which to say mass. They also began to raise money from their congregations, and by other means, in order to begin building permanent chapels. The rest of the money would be borrowed, and once the chapel was completed the debt would be paid off over the years. In Paisley,

St Mirrin's was opened in 1809 and St Mary's, Greenock, in 1816. Ayr was not so fortunate. In 1814 its priest died without either he or his two predecessors having been able to erect a chapel. Furthermore, a shortage of clergymen within the Catholic Church resulted in the Ayr mission being deprived of a permanent priest until 1823, when William Thomson was sent there. In the intervening period the priests from Glasgow, Greenock, and Paisley paid visits to the town to say mass, but no further progress was made with regard to the establishment of a chapel. This changed once Thomson was stationed in the town. He took to his task with great zeal and as a result St Margaret's chapel was opened in 1827.[5] Missions were also established in Wigtownshire in 1825, and at Dumbarton in 1829. Churches were opened there in 1832 and 1830 respectively. By the mid-1830s the size of the congregation of all these missions was as follows: Paisley, c.6–8,000;[6] Ayr, c.5–6,000;[7] Greenock, c.4–6,000;[8] Dumbarton, c.1,000;[9] Wigtownshire, c.3,000[10]. Each mission had one priest, except for Greenock, which had two, one of whom was Bishop Scott, Vicar Apostolic of the Western District.[11]

Despite the progress which had undoubtedly been made by the Catholic Church in the western lowland counties during this period of Irish immigration, there was still an under-provision of priests and chapels. This shortage becomes even more apparent when one considers that the congregation of each mission in the mid-1830s did not all live in the towns where their chapels were located. For example, 43–44,000 of the 50,000 Catholics of the Glasgow Mission resided in the city and its suburbs or within two miles of the city. Most of the remainder lived in towns and villages throughout Lanarkshire, with numbers resident even as far distant as Lanark. Small groups of Catholics in parts of Renfrewshire, Dumbartonshire, and Stirlingshire were also attached to the Glasgow Mission.[12] Elsewhere the situation was even more serious: only one half of the congregation of the Paisley Mission actually lived in the town itself: the rest were scattered throughout the parishes of Renfrewshire, in towns and villages such as Neilston, Crofthead, Barrhead, Nitshill, Elderslie, Linwood, Johnston, Lochwinnoch, Kilbarchan, Bridge of Weir, Houston, Renfrew;[13] the Ayr Mission embraced almost all of the

Catholics living in the county of Ayrshire; for example, at Kilmarnock, Girvan, Maybole, Saltcoats, Irvine, Ardrossan, and Troon;[14] the congregation of the Greenock Mission was composed of the Catholics of that town and those at places such as Port Glasgow, Gourock, Inverkip, Largs, West Kilbride;[15] the priest at Newton-Stewart, Richard Sinnot, was in charge of the Catholics scattered throughout the whole of Wigtownshire as well as some of those who lived in the western part of Kirkcudbrightshire. In total, his mission extended over an area of nearly 1,000 square miles.[16]

Naturally, this was not an ideal situation for either congregation or priest. Many Catholics, for example, had to walk considerable distances in order to attend mass. The clergymen tried to deal with this problem by occasionally holding services at some of the more distant towns in which members of their congregations resided. For example, during the 1830s William Thomson, priest at Ayr, said mass every sixth or eighth Sunday at Girvan, and at Irvine and Kilmarnock every fourth Sunday alternately.[17] Richard Sinnot said mass at stated times in certain places in his Wigtownshire mission.[18] The congregations who attended such services would assemble in rented halls. Yet, despite such measures, those who wished to fulfil their religious duties on a more regular, or even weekly basis, would ultimately have to make the long journey to and from the mission church.[19] In addition to travelling to the out-stations to say mass, the priests of the missions in the western lowlands had to make other lengthy excursions, such as when they visited the sick of their congregations who lived far from the church, or when they made other visits to such areas in the course of their pastoral duties.[20] This state of affairs was of great concern to the clergy. John Bremner, priest of the Paisley Mission, stated in January 1838 that his congregation was 'too numerous and much too scattered to be properly superintended by one individual'.[21] The report of the Glasgow Mission in the *Scottish Catholic Directory* for 1831 concluded that it was 'very evident that the present number of chapels and clergymen must be very inadequate to the spiritual wants of the congregation . . . '. In the same edition, Richard Sinnot reported that one priest and one chapel were inadequate for the needs of his Wigtownshire mission: several of both were required.[22] By the mid-1830s, ten priests and seven chapels were clearly not sufficient to deal effectively with the spiritual needs of the seventy thousand Irish Catholics who lived in the western lowland counties of Scotland.

The financial position of the Catholic Church in these areas was responsible for these shortages. In the early 1830s most of the missions were still paying off the debts on their chapels. By 1831 the debt on St Mirrin's, Paisley stood at £1,700. At the same time heavy debts remained on the chapels at Glasgow and Ayr.[23] The revenue of the missions came mainly from the weekly contributions and other donations from their congregations. This income was used to meet the expenses of the priests and the mission and to service the debt.[24] No surplus funds were available to the clergy to build new chapels or procure more priests for the western lowland missions.[25] Furthermore, the poverty of the Irish Catholic congregations in this period was such that their Scottish clergymen were unable to raise any additional revenue from them.[26]

The poor financial condition of these missions can be further demonstrated by the history of some of their schools. Until 1817 there were no Catholic schools in Glasgow, as its priests could not afford to establish any. In October of that year a Catholic Schools' Society was formed in the city to provide the means of education for the Catholic children. The organisation consisted of members of the Catholic congregation and of members of the Protestant community, and its chairman was the city's Member of Parliament, Kirkman Finlay. By 1830 the society had established five Catholic schools in the city, and these were chiefly financed by the contributions of Protestant subscribers. The pupils paid a fee of a penny a week. Those whose families could not afford this amount were admitted free. The support of the city's benevolent Protestants, however, came at a price. Although the teachers were Catholics, they were not permitted to give their pupils instruction in the Catholic religion. In addition, the Protestant version of the Bible was used in classes. The Glasgow priests were not in a position to refuse these conditions.[27]

During the early 1830s the schools established by the Society were in financial difficulty. Indeed the account of the Glasgow Mission in the *Scottish Catholic Directory* in 1831 reported that they were 'in a manner struggling for existence, in consequence of the want of funds, the subscriptions which once were very considerable, having dwindled into an insignificant sum'. The report went on to state that the poverty of the city's Catholics was such that they could provide little financial assistance, and it further explained that because of the need to service the debt contracted in the erection of St Andrew's chapel, the Glasgow Mission had little or no funds to spare to provide for Catholic schools.[28] The *Catholic Directories* for 1832 to 1835 reprinted this report.[29]

Protestant support was also vital for the establishment of a Catholic School in Paisley in 1816. The school was supervised by a committee of twelve Catholics and twelve Protestants, and financed partly by subscriptions and partly through the fees of the pupils. As in Glasgow, conditions were laid down by the Protestant benefactors. The Catholic religion was not taught and the King James version of the Bible was used for scripture reading. The School Committee had the right to inspect the school when it wished. By the 1830s there were two other Catholic schools in Paisley, although these were neither established nor supported by the School Committee, but were financed solely by the fees of the students.[30]

The one Catholic school at Greenock was maintained without any outside assistance. It depended on the fees of the pupils as well as on contributions from the Catholics in the town. When the school was opened in 1818 the then priest, John Davidson, met with some of Greenock's Protestants, but they would not support the school unless Davidson abandoned religious instruction. This he refused to do, a stance which other priests could not afford to take.[31]

The mission at Ayr had neither Protestant benefactors nor a congregation with sufficient means to provide for the education of its Catholic children. In early 1823 William Thomson opened a school in the town, but it eventually had to close through lack of finances.[32] The *Catholic Directory* for 1831 stated of Ayr that 'several attempts have been made to establish a school, but have unfortunately failed: the people are unable to pay for their children and there are no funds to support a schoolmaster'.[33] It was not until 1856 that Thomson was finally able to establish lasting Catholic schools in the town.[34]

The immigration of Irish Catholics to the west of Scotland from the mid-1790s placed the Catholic Church under immense pressure. The church was not wealthy and could only send priests to the region when they became available. Chapels were erected only when sufficient funds had been collected to begin construction, and where there was a congregation large enough to be able, through its weekly contributions, to help repay the money borrowed to complete the building. By the mid-1830s, however, progress had been made. Chapels and priests were present in the western lowlands. Yet there was still an under-provision of both. The debts incurred in the establishment of places of worship, along with the poverty of the church and the immigrants, prevented the establishment of new missions, the building of new churches, and the acquisition of more priests. This critical state of affairs placed a great strain on both the clergymen and their congregations.

Yet, the subsequent decade or so was, by contrast, a period of rapid expansion for the Catholic Church in the western lowlands. By the end of 1848 ten new missions had been established in the region and in six of these chapels were built. The Glasgow Mission also grew. St Mary's in Abercrombie Street was opened in 1842; the Gorbals chapel in Portugal Street was enlarged and renovated and re-opened as St John's on the first Sunday of Lent, 1846. A chapel house and two schools were built alongside it. Later that year St Alphonsus was opened. This was originally a dissenting Protestant church, which had been purchased for the Glasgow Mission by Bishop John Murdoch the previous year. The number of priests increased along with this expansion in the number of missions and chapels: by the end of 1848 there were, apart from Bishops Murdoch and Smith, thirty-two priests serving in the western lowlands.[35]

An improvement in the financial condition of the church in the Western District was responsible for the beginning of this growth. In 1835 Bishop Murdoch resolved to liquidate the heavy debt on

St Andrew's church in Glasgow. He organised weekly collections for this purpose, and by 1840 the debt was paid off. This meant that a sizeable portion of the future income of St Andrew's was not lost to the mission. It may also have been the case that Murdoch's collection raised surplus funds to help establish new missions and erect new chapels.[36] Another collection at this time raised a substantial amount for the District. In 1839 Peter Forbes, one of the priests at Glasgow, received permission from Bishop Scott to go on a begging tour of the south of Ireland to raise funds for the establishment of new chapels. He left Scotland in 1839 and returned with around £3,000.[37]

Such an increase in income was of great benefit to the Catholic Church. It allowed land to be purchased for chapels to be built on and it also aided the construction of them. New churches and missions would be pointless, however, without clergymen to staff them. The improved state of its funds also allowed the church to procure more priests for the District. There were not sufficient numbers in Scotland and so many were recruited from Ireland: sixteen of the thirty-two priests active in the western lowlands in 1848 were Irish. From 1838, when they were first used, until the end of 1849 a total of thirty-five Irish priests served in the Western District.[38]

It had been apparent by the mid-1830s that new missions, chapels and priests were desperately needed. But they had to be financed. There was no point in establishing a mission and placing priests at it, or in erecting a chapel, if the congregation of the mission was not of sufficient numbers or means to offer financial support to these developments in the long term. Some areas were clearly able to do this by the middle of the 1830s, and when money and priests became available, new missions and churches were soon established. This was the case in Glasgow and also in Renfrewshire: for example, a mission was established in Barrhead in 1839 and a chapel opened there in 1842; the previous year St Fillan's was opened in Houston.

Other areas came to have sufficient numbers over the period 1834–48. It is no coincidence that the five new missions established in Ayrshire and Lanarkshire during these years were situated in towns and villages at the heart of areas in which these counties' rapidly expanding coal and iron industries were located. These districts attracted large numbers of Irish workers as a result of these developments.[39] In Ayrshire a mission was established at Kilmarnock in 1845 and a church opened two years later, at which time the congregation, located in the town and in surrounding districts, numbered about 3,000.[40] In 1845 a mission was also established at Dalry. The *Scottish Catholic Directory* for 1846 reported that this was because of the great and rapid 'increase of Catholics over a large tract of country, in the centre of which the village of Dalry is situated . . . '.[41] In Lanarkshire priests from Glasgow said mass at regular intervals at Airdrie throughout the 1830s. In 1833 the Catholic population there was around eight hundred: by 1838 the number had risen to an estimated eleven hundred.[42] St Margaret's was opened in the town the following year, and in 1842 its priest had almost five thousand in his congregation.[43] The number of Irish workers in the area's coal and iron works continued to grow to such an extent that the Airdrie Mission was divided in 1845 and another established at Coatbridge.[44] By 1850 the congregation at Airdrie was estimated at around six thousand and that of Coatbridge at five thousand.[45] The missions at Airdrie and Coatbridge were two of the three established in Lanarkshire during this period. The other was at Hamilton.

The Establishment of the Hamilton Mission

In September 1843 John Scanlan, an Irish priest who had come to Scotland the previous year, arrived in Hamilton and took up residence in a cottage in Almada Street. He had been sent to the town to establish the mission. There was no chapel in Hamilton although ground had been obtained as a site for both chapel and chapel house. No money was available to begin building; it was Scanlan's responsibility to raise the necessary funds, and he soon began his collection. In the meantime, services were held in a hired hall.[46]

Prior to Scanlan's arrival, mass had been said in the town at regular intervals for some time by visiting priests. It is not known exactly when this first began but it was probably either late 1826 or early 1827.[47] In February 1827, John Murdoch, one of the Glasgow priests, informed a colleague that one of the clergymen in the city said mass at Hamilton once a month to a congregation of around five hundred.[48] This continued to be the arrangement until January 1831 when services were cut back to once every six weeks, in order to enable one of the Glasgow priests to officiate to the more numerous body of Catholics of Airdrie, also once in the six weeks.[49] Both congregations paid the expenses of the priests and hired the halls in which the mass was said. In Hamilton the Mason's Hall was rented for this purpose.[50] Until 1838 these were the only towns in Lanarkshire in which the Glasgow priests held services.[51] From 1836 Mass was said more frequently in both towns, as the priests came every three weeks.[52] At Hamilton, three to four hundred people usually attended these services during the 1830s, and according to one informed estimate this would represent a Catholic congregation of over one thousand.[53] In the early 1840s, until Scanlan's arrival, Glasgow priests continued to hold regular services in the town, except for a short period when the priest from the recently established Airdrie Mission officiated.[54]

It would be wrong to assume that those who attended the services of the Glasgow priests between 1827 and 1843, or those who subsequently formed Scanlan's congregation, resided in the town itself or even in the parish. The Catholics of the Hamilton Mission were scattered over a dozen civil parishes in Lanarkshire, in towns and villages such as Stonehouse, Motherwell, Strathaven, East Kilbride, Blantyre, Chapelton, Bothwell, Bellshill, Uddingston, Newarthill, Carfin, Mossend, Cleland, Larkhall, Dalziel, Wishaw, Carluke, Carnwath, Lanark, and so on.[55] Those who attended mass in the town prior to Scanlan's arrival no doubt also came from these areas, given that the only other place in Lanarkshire in which mass was said at the time was Airdrie.

Once settled in the town Scanlan began collecting for the Hamilton Chapel. Not only did he raise money from his congregation, he also made successful begging trips to Edinburgh, Dundee, and Aberdeen. Unfortunately, the funds he accumulated were not applied to the purpose for which they were collected. In April 1845 Scanlan took off with all the money. He made his way to Liverpool and from there sailed to America.[56] According to Bishop Scott the chapel funds were not all that Scanlan had stolen:

> . . . he carried with him £17 belonging to a poor man who a few months before had lodged it in his hands for safety. He borrowed money from different people under some pretence or other and £20 from a Protestant woman, all of which he took with him. He also swindled a Catholic traveler [sic] out of a gold watch worth £30. She was not sold to him, but he asked the traveler to leave the watch with him for a few days till he would show her to, and have the opinion, of a friend of his of the quality of the watch. But without consulting his friend he took her with him to America.

Scott also informed Bishop Kyle that Scanlan left a 'great deal of debt in Hamilton' and that he was afraid that the creditors would 'seize the furniture in the house occupied by [Scanlan], though it was bought for, and paid by the people, for that Mission whoever should be Missionary there'.[57] Michael Condon, in charge of the Hamilton Mission from 1850 to 1859, suggests in his account of the mission that personal difficulties were the cause of Scanlan's sudden departure.[58]

Scanlan's successor at Hamilton was another Irish priest, James Purcell. Purcell had come to Scotland in 1838 and had initially served at St Mirrin's in Paisley. When St John's Barrhead opened in October 1841 he was given charge of it and remained there until his removal to Hamilton.[59] During his time at the Hamilton Mission the building of the chapel and priest's house commenced. The cost of this, along with the chapel ground, was over £2,000.[60] The *Catholic Directory* for 1846 reported that Purcell was in the process of collecting funds for the construction of the chapel, but admitted that 'Notwithstanding all his exertions it will remain encumbered with a heavy debt.'[61] No doubt his task was made all the more difficult by the memory of the activities of his predecessor. Purcell, however, did not remain in Hamilton long enough to see the chapel completed. Having to minister to Catholics scattered over such a large area of Lanarkshire was evidently too much for him: Michael Condon recalled of Purcell that 'finding himself unequal to the long rides and desires of the Mission, he resigned and returned to Ireland, in August 1846. He was a good priest; but too corpulent for missionary labour'.[62] His collection and a grant from the Scottish Catholic Church however, enabled the debt to be reduced to £1,500.[63]

Purcell was replaced by a Scottish priest, James Smith, who, since his ordination in 1842, had served in Glasgow at St Andrew's.[64] Shortly after his arrival in Hamilton, St Mary's church was opened on 29 November 1846. The chapel had seats for six hundred people, and the priest's house was connected to it.[65] Unfortunately, Smith's period in charge of the Hamilton Mission was not a successful one. According to Michael Condon, for the first eight months of 1847 Smith was 'unable . . . to recite the Divine Office'.[66] It is not known why this was the case. On hearing of this Bishop Murdoch sent William Burke, a recently ordained priest from Ireland, to assist him. He remained at the mission for eight months.[67] After Burke departed for Dalry, Smith occasionally received help from the priests at Glasgow. Despite this the work of the mission became too great for him. Not only had he to minister to the widely dispersed congregation which attended St Mary's, he also had to attend to the Catholics who lived in the upper ward of Lanarkshire: Smith said mass at regular intervals at Carluke, Lanark, Carnwath, and Auchingray. This continued until May 1849 when a priest was sent to Lanark to establish a mission there.[68]

By May 1850 Smith had been unable to reduce the chapel debt. This may have been partly caused by the loss of income as a result of the establishment of the Lanark Mission, a general drop in revenue from his congregation, as a result of trade depressions, and also because William Burke's salary and expenses had to be paid for during his stay as assistant priest.[69] It would appear, however, that Smith was not particularly adept at managing the finances of the Hamilton Mission. According to Condon, Smith had received a gift of £250 from Robert Monteith, a wealthy Catholic convert, and had 'resold a part of the chapel ground for £150, and had, in one year alone, an income of £800 . . . '. Furthermore, after he no longer had to say mass in the upper ward of Lanarkshire, he still continued to use mission funds for the hire of a gig and to pay for the upkeep of his horse. The money expended on these was not inconsiderable.[70] In order to extricate the mission from its dire financial position Smith embarked on a begging tour.

Smith's temporary replacement was Michael Condon, an Irish priest who was to play a crucial role in the development of the Hamilton Mission.[71] He arrived in the town on 23 May and found a mission that was very much run down. Smith had not left any funds for his replacement and so Condon had to use his own money to pay for food for himself, the housekeeper (who was Smith's sister), the servant, a dog and some canaries. At his first mass, on 26 May, he 'preached to a very sparse congregation'.[72] Condon later recalled that his period as assistant priest was a particularly difficult one:

> During those six months my toils and trials, at Hamilton, were hot and heavy. Being merely Mr Smith's substitute, I could neither correct nor control expenditure and other abuses; nor project any improvements. The chapel was bare of ornament; and the house of furniture. There was no school. In consequence of the frequent illnesses of Mr Smith on Sundays, the people cased [*sic*] to come to chapel, or contribute.[73]

Condon also had to make numerous visits to the sick among his congregation. He estimated that the total distance covered by his journeys to the areas outside Hamilton and its vicinity was around three hundred miles. Unfortunately, he had not his own transport, and Smith had sold his horse prior to Condon's arrival. Around one-third of the distance Condon travelled in making these calls was by gig, bus, or train; he walked the remainder in order to save the mission money.[74] Despite the problems he faced, Condon had some successes during Smith's absence. He established Sunday schools at Strathaven, Cleland, Wishaw, and Carfin, and, by visiting his congregation and urging them to attend to their religious duties, he was able to increase the attendance at Sunday mass from around one hundred to five times that number.[75]

By the autumn of 1850 Smith, who was in England, had neither contacted Bishop Murdoch nor sent him any funds from his begging expedition. This greatly angered Murdoch who re-called him to Hamilton, and even threatened to suspend Smith if he did not come immediately. Smith eventually returned on 9 November 1850 with only £10 to show for his six months' stay south of the border. This convinced Murdoch that Smith was not fit to be the priest of a mission such as Hamilton. On 26 November Smith was transferred to Newton Stewart. Condon was made his successor.[76]

The Condon Years, 1850–1859

Michael Condon was born on 23 September 1817 at Craves, Coolcappa, in County Limerick. Between 1841 and 1845 he attended St Mary's Seminary, Youghal, County Cork, and then All Hallows in Dublin. He was ordained in Glasgow on 6 October 1845 and became one of the assistant priests at St Mary's in Calton. Condon soon found himself ministering to the poor, fever-stricken Irish of the city, and eventually fell seriously ill as a result. Once recovered from the epidemic he was sent, in the summer of 1847, to take charge of the Campbeltown Mission in Argyllshire. His congregation was scattered over a huge area, including the islands of Jura, Arran, and Islay. During his period there he oversaw the construction of St Kieran's, and made numerous begging expeditions to raise money for his mission. In total he raised over £900 and was able to clear the debt on his chapel.[77]

During his stays in Glasgow, in Campbeltown, and in Hamilton prior to Smith's removal, Condon had established himself as an honest, hard-working, and dedicated clergyman, and also one who could effectively run a large mission. These, no doubt, were the reasons why Murdoch decided to keep Condon at Hamilton. The mission was not, however, one which Condon desired. For example, in his account of his time at Hamilton he recalls his feelings when he first arrived in the town in May 1850:

> After the fever years of Glasgow and my journeying for Campbeltown, I fondly thought my missionary labours might end. I coveted but some quiet corner where I might pass a few years and

die. Instead of this I found myself in the most important, extensive and withal embarrassed, country Mission in Scotland.[78]

His period as substitute priest in Hamilton did not, apparently, alter his opinion; in November 1850 he begged Bishop Murdoch not to remove James Smith from his position in charge of the mission.[79] Murdoch was certainly aware that Condon's new position was an unenviable one. In a letter dated 16 February 1851 Murdoch told him that:

> You have been placed in a difficult position . . . No doubt you have an arduous task before you . . . The piece of work allotted to you, I mean the rescue of a nearly ruined Mission, is not to be done by a vigorous effort of brief duration. In order to complete it, you will have to toil and struggle for years . . . a noble deed it will be in the sight of God, if you retrieve affairs at Hamilton . . . I beg you to understand that I commit the Mission to you *unconditionally*; I fix no salary, no amount for house support, no amount for anything . . . You are not to lose courage.[80]

Although Condon had not wanted to remain at Hamilton he was not one to retreat from the challenge which faced him, as he later recalled: 'Having now unfettered controul [*sic*] of this ruined Mission, I resolved to rescue it even at sacrifice of my life.'[81] Condon was to remain in charge of the mission until May 1859.

He began by reorganising the affairs of the mission. One of his first actions was to take a detailed census of his congregation. The number in each parish was as follows: Hamilton 746; Shotts 392; Bothwell 342; Blantyre 298; Avondale 211; Cambusnethan 94; Dalziel 71; Dalserf 20; Kilbride 17; Glassford 7; Stonehouse 2. The number of Catholics attached to the Hamilton Mission was therefore 2,200, with five of the eleven parishes having 1,999 members of the congregation.[82] On 16 February 1851 Condon called a meeting of the mission and formed a chapel committee whose task was to liquidate the debt on St Mary's. Collectors were appointed for the various parishes in which the congregation resided. At this meeting Sunday school monitors were appointed and the choir reconstituted.[83] Condon's congregation was almost exclusively working class. The *Glasgow Free Press* of November 1852 gives the following description of the Irish Catholics of the Hamilton Mission:

In Strathaven they dig drains. In Bothwell, Uddingston, Stonehouse and Larkhall they labour in the fields. In Blantyre they work at the cotton mills or dyeworks. In Bellshill, Jerviestown [*sic*], Newarthill, Carfin, Wishaw and Rumblingseike they make bricks or mine at the iron or the coal. In Cleland they toil at the pig-iron furnaces, and at Hamilton, whilst a few live as brokers, the great majority support life by vending delph, fish, whiting, or exchanging them to the country people for rags, bones, old iron, etc.[84]

Until the summer of 1854 Condon was the sole priest at the Hamilton Mission. He had a heavy workload, as the following account of his travels in 1852 demonstrates:

Besides thirty trips to Glasgow, five to Coatbridge, two to Arran, two to Carstairs, 2 to Lanark and 1 each to Greenock, Barrhead and Airdrie and my numerous calls and avocations in and about Hamilton, I had moreover in 1852, 70 sick calls, averaging over 11 miles each and representing a total of 778 miles to the outlying towns, villages and hamlets. Only to 100 of the 788 miles had I any chance of conveyances, bus, train or gig, a total cost to the Mission of 11s. 11d. While I had the remaining 670 miles to travel on foot. On my way to and from any such calls I had often to attend several sick persons.

These calls to the outposts were to Cleland 14; Cleland and Wishaw 1; Cleland and Newarthill 1; Cleland and Blantyre; Cleland, Newarthill and Mothwerwell 1; Strathaven 11; Strathaven and Carfin 1; Wishaw 4; Bellshill 2; Jerriston [*sic*] and Rumblingsike [*sic*] 1; Aikintubber 3; Blantyre 4; Blantyre and Motherwell 1; Newarthill 4; Larkhall 1; Ratcock 2; Skeagh; Uddingston 1; Carfin 2; Croftbasket 2 . . . [85]

Condon walked to so many sick calls in order to save the mission money. He did so to great personal discomfort: 'My feet were often blistered and sometimes bleeding; but somehow they soon healed.'[86] Although the average distance he travelled on such visits was between ten and twelve miles,[87] sometimes the journeys were of considerable length. In 1852 a sick call to Strathaven and Carfin on the same day resulted in a twenty-four mile walk.[88] The previous year, on 27 October, saw Condon walk to Wishaw, Strathaven, and Cleland, and then to the army barracks where Catholic soldiers were stationed – a total distance of forty miles.[89] Such dedicated missionary labour greatly touched the Catholics of the Hamilton Mission. At the beginning of December 1853 they gave Condon a gig and a month later provided him with a horse. On 31 January 1854 these, together with two sets of harness, were formally presented to Condon at a service held in the Mason's Hall in Hamilton which was attended by over 300 members of his congregation. The total cost of these gifts was £70.[90] The gift of the horse and the gig came at a very fortuitous time for Condon as an epidemic of cholera soon broke out throughout the various towns, villages, and country areas of the Hamilton Mission. It lasted for most of 1854.[91] Condon's already heavy workload was greatly increased:

> I got little rest, night or day. I wd be no sooner home from one call, than I wd have to start to another, either to the same spot, or elsewhere. The longest of the days calls might not be more than 40 miles – but their ceaselessness was worrying and their suddeness a source of perpetual anxiety to priest and patient.[92]

March was a particularly difficult month for Condon. He recalled that during that period the tramp of his horse 'was heard, here, there and everywhere, both night and day'.[93] Indeed, his labours that month were so great that the Catholics of the mission sent a deputation to Bishop Murdoch and asked him to send an assistant priest to St Mary's. Murdoch, however, had 'not the limb of a priest to spare', but offered his own services to Condon for day work, in order to leave Condon fresh for the calls to cholera victims at night.[94] A rather embarrassed Condon declined Murdoch's offer: 'I wrote to say I had nothing to do with the deputation, and that he need have no anxiety for me, until he shd. hear myself complain.'[95]

It did not, of course, take an epidemic of cholera to convince Condon, his congregation, and Bishop Murdoch that one priest was insufficient for the needs of the Hamilton Mission. Unfortunately, since William Burke's removal to Dalry in May 1848, the number of clergymen under Murdoch's charge had not increased to a sufficient level to enable him to provide Hamilton with another assistant priest.[96] Even if one had become available during this period, the precarious financial condition of the Hamilton Mission could have made it impossible for him to be stationed at St Mary's. The following extract from a letter to

Condon from Bishop Murdoch, dated 5 December 1853, illustrates this point:

> You will have the first priest at my command. Perhaps it is as well that you shd be without one for a time, till you see what additional expense the keeping of a horse is to cause you. I am not without fear that you will not be able for a coadjutor and a horse too. If possible a certain amount of the debt must be paid every year.[97]

The following June, Murdoch wrote to Condon and informed him that he had finally been able to procure another priest for the Hamilton Mission. He was Patrick O'Leary, an Irish priest who had been ordained two years previously.[98] This news undoubtedly came as a great relief to Condon, for cholera was still rife throughout the various districts where his congregation resided,[99] and his workload around this time was just as heavy as it had been earlier in the year:

> My cholera calls were still incessant. No sooner had I returned from one than I was off to another. Night or day, weekday, or Sunday, there was no rest for me or my poor horse. He was growing heavy on the hoof, and I on the saddle or the gig.[100]

O'Leary arrived in Hamilton in June 1854 and remained for one year. Unfortunately, his period as assistant priest proved to be something of a nightmare for Condon. In his account of the Hamilton Mission he describes O'Leary as 'a gloomy, unprincipled man, of truculent temper and lax moral'. Prior to his posting to St Mary's he had been discovered, at St Andrew's chapel in Glasgow, reading Bishop Smith's private letters. O'Leary's services were then offered to two of the priests at Glasgow, Patrick Hanley and James Danaher, clergymen at St Patrick's and St Joseph's respectively, 'but they, warned by Irish friends, wd have nothing to do with him'. Murdoch then sent O'Leary to Condon, who knew nothing of the character of his new assistant.[101] It did not take him long to find out. It would appear that O'Leary took an instant dislike to Condon. He publicly criticised his parish priest, and would occasionally refuse to sit at breakfast with Condon, preferring to eat alone later.[102] At the end of 1854 he refused to make some calls to the sick, even though it was his turn to do so. Condon went instead.[103] It was around this time that O'Leary first made a number of allegations and insinuations about Condon's conduct at Hamilton. He repeated them the following February. On both occasions Condon complained to Murdoch, who investigated the matter and found that the charges were false. O'Leary was made to apologise to Condon. In June he again repeated his accusations and also made new ones. They too were shown to be spurious. This time O'Leary had gone too far. Although he tried to retract his allegations an exasperated Bishop Murdoch withdrew O'Leary's faculties and ordered him to leave the Western District.[104]

O'Leary's successor at Hamilton was James Milne, a recently ordained Scottish priest, who was also the nephew of Bishop Murdoch. He arrived at the mission in the autumn of 1855.[105] For over two years his stay at Hamilton passed without incident. In March 1858, however, Milne criticised, from the pulpit on a Sunday, the recruiting tactics of the military stationed in the town. One of the consequences of Milne's outburst was that Catholic soldiers were not permitted to attend mass at St Mary's as long as Milne officiated there. In June Murdoch promised the War Office that he would remove Milne, and in August he sent him to St Mungo's in Glasgow. Murdoch believed that Milne should not have become embroiled in a public dispute with the military.[106] Financial considerations may also have influenced Murdoch's decision. The Hamilton Mission, along with several others in which there were military stations, received payments from the War Office for ministering to the Catholic soldiers and for accommodating them at mass. Furthermore, since January 1858, Condon and the priests of these other missions, had been petitioning the War Office for an increase in their remunerations. They received only five shillings per man, per annum, whereas Episcopal clergymen were paid double that rate for providing similar services to members of their religion. Presbyterian ministers received seven shillings and six pence a man per annum. Condon and his colleagues requested that their rate be raised to that of their Episcopal counterparts. A similar movement was taking place in England. In June 1858 the War Office equalised payments for clergymen of all denominations and as a result the income from this source doubled for Condon and the other Catholic clergymen.[107]

Murdoch replaced Milne with James McCafferty, a recently ordained priest from Buncrana, County Donegal. Condon describes him as 'a squat, crafty, and selfishly mean little man'.[108] He states that McCafferty 'often absented himself, for days and nights, without leave. He borrowed money; or bought and sent goods to Buncrana, without paying for them'.[109] Condon's opinion of his assistant was apparently not shared by the congregation of the Hamilton Mission. When McCafferty left St Mary's in November 1859 to found the Strathaven Mission, he received a presentation address from the Catholics of Hamilton which praised him for his labours among the congregation: 'Your time in Hamilton was not so lengthened as we could desire but was sufficiently long to prove to us the sterling value of your heart and mind . . . We allude to your untiring and devoted efforts in matters of education . . . You have been constantly at your post of duty . . . '[110]

Despite the problems and differences Condon had with his assistant priests their presence at Hamilton from 1854 meant that the work of the mission was shared. Condon's missionary labours did not, however, decrease as a result. This can be demonstrated, for example, by his visits to the sick of his congregation who lived out with Hamilton and its immediate neighbourhood. In 1851 he made 76 calls; in 1852, 70; in 1853, 65. In 1855 he made 95 visits; in 1856, 80; in 1857, 114, and in 1858, 92. His assistants made similar numbers of calls.[111] Condon's workload did not become lighter simply because the number of Catholics in the Hamilton Mission dramatically increased during the 1850s. In 1851 his census of the mission established that there were 2,200 members of his congregation. In 1857 Condon took another census which he completed in October of that year. It revealed that in just six years the Roman Catholic population of the Hamilton Mission had more than doubled, to 4,474 persons. The number in each civil parish was as follows: Hamilton, 1411; Bothwell, 856; Shotts, 840; Cambusnethan, 379; Avodale, 319; Blantyre, 307; Dalziel, 256; Dalserf, 95; Stonehouse, 11.[112] This growth of the Hamilton congregation was not solely caused by natural increase. Many Irish workers came to this part of Lanarkshire during this period and found employment in the iron works, the coal mines, and in the construction of railway lines.[113] Indeed, in March 1858, five months after Condon's second census, work began on a new line of railway at Strathaven, and according to Condon the influx of workers to the area increased his congregation to around 5,000.[114]

During his time at St Mary's Condon opened mission stations at Strathaven and Cleland. He was not, however, able to do so until some time after he took charge of the Hamilton Mission. The station at Strathaven was established in December 1853. By this time around three hundred members of Condon's congregation lived in and around this village, which is eight miles from Hamilton. To attend mass at St Mary's these people had to travel farther than most of the other Catholics attached to the Hamilton Mission. Furthermore, the chapel had become overcrowded on Sundays. A station at Strathaven had not been established prior to this because Condon had not his own means of transport. This changed with the gift from his congregation of the horse and gig. In December 1853 he hired a hall in the village to serve as both chapel and schoolroom for the Catholics of Strathaven and its neighbourhood. On the eleventh of that month he drove there and held his first Sunday service. He then returned to St Mary's and said his second mass of the day. Thereafter Condon did this every month until June 1854 when O'Leary arrived at the mission. The presence of two priests at St Mary's resulted in mass being said at Strathaven once a fortnight; and this continued until Strathaven became a separate mission in late 1859.[115]

Prior to the establishment of the station at Strathaven, Condon had unsuccessfully tried for some time to open one at Cleland, where a large number of his congregation resided. Eventually he managed to obtain the use of a schoolhouse located next to the Cleland Iron Works. Both were owned by Robert Stewart, Lord Provost of Glasgow. Mass was said in the room for the first time on New Year's Day 1854. Towards the end of January and before another service was held, the use of the premises was withdrawn by Stewart after he was informed that his agreement had aroused local opposition. The following December he changed his mind and once again allowed Condon to hold Sunday services in the schoolroom. The first took place on 31 December. From then on mass was said at Cleland on alternate Sundays with Strathaven.[116]

When Condon arrived in Hamilton in May 1850 there was no Catholic school in any of the towns and villages of the mission, nor had there been since the establishment of the mission in 1843. Lack of funds had been the cause of this. Once in charge at St Mary's Condon was powerless to alter this situation: 'The Mission debt, with its heavy annual interest, forbade any attempt at opening a Catholic school.'[117] Members of his congregation frequently asked him if they could establish a school, but Condon was unable to give them permission: 'I found the applicants so ignorant that I had to refuse.'[118] He eventually allowed a teacher to open a school in November 1851, but was unable to provide him with any financial support. The teacher closed the school the following May, as the fees of the pupils were insufficient to pay his salary.[119]

In January 1853, however, the Catholic school at Hamilton was finally opened. Funding came from what at the time seemed an unlikely source. In December 1852 Condon met the Duchess of Hamilton, who made many enquiries about his mission. Afterwards she gave Condon £20 to establish his school. He believed that the Duchess was simply concerned about the poor state of affairs of the mission.[120] The following August, however, she revealed to Condon that she had converted to Catholicism in 1850 – two years before her husband inherited the Dukedom.[121] Condon opened the school on 17 January 1853. Around one-third of the contribution of the Duchess was used to purchase items for the schoolroom, such as a clock, a desk, globes, and maps. The remainder paid the teacher's salary, which was 'supplemented by the moderate fees of 2d., or 1d. each, weekly, from the pupils'.[122] Thereafter, the Duchess made an annual donation of £20 towards the upkeep of the school.[123] During Condon's period in charge of the Hamilton Mission the school was attended during the day by around sixty boys and girls, and at night by perhaps half that number.[124] In the 1850s there were also Sunday schools at Hamilton, Strathaven, Motherwell, Carfin, Cleland,

Wishaw, and other towns and villages throughout the mission. At these the children would receive religious instruction from the clergymen at St Mary's.[125]

The annual gift of £20 for the school was not all that the Duchess gave to the Hamilton Mission during Condon's time in charge. She donated statues, vestments, vases, candlesticks, cruets, altar liners, chalices, medals, crosses, amongst other items for St Mary's.[126] She also gave Condon money for a set of stations of the cross, a new altar for the chapel, and two side altars.[127] In September 1852 the Duchess gave Condon £20 which he used to contribute towards the cost of installing gas in the chapel and chapel house.[128] The Duchess attended services at St Mary's, and when she stayed in Arran Condon would journey there to give her mass.[129]

The gifts and donations of the Duchess of Hamilton, and those from aristocratic visitors to Hamilton Palace, such as the Count and Countess de Villeneuve-Arifet,[130] were, of course, welcomed by Condon. The money gifts were usually given to pay for certain items, e.g., altars, carpets, stations of the cross. The £20 annual donation from the Duchess was for the support of the Catholic school. Such gifts, along with the payments from the War Office and the money received from the Western District Fund, should not disguise the fact that the vast bulk of the income of the Hamilton Mission came from the contributions of the congregation, which was overwhelmingly composed of Irish workers.[131] These took the form of collections at mass, the renting of seats at St Mary's, money given at baptisms and weddings and special collections. Income from these sources rose during Condon's period at Hamilton, no doubt because of the doubling of his congregation: in 1851 his receipts from his congregation came to around £200; in 1858 it amounted to c.£420.[132] The income of the Hamilton Mission was used to pay the salaries of Condon and his assistants; the wages of the housekeepers, the servants, and the teachers; taxes; feu duties; repairs; housekeeping, and other expenses associated with the management of the Hamilton Mission. Before Condon acquired a horse and gig money was necessary to pay for transport: afterwards it was used for the upkeep of the horse, as well as for longer journeys, for example, to Arran. Funds had to be allocated to pay the debt and interest on St Mary's chapel. When Condon took over the mission the debt stood at £1,700: through careful management of income and expenditure he managed to reduce it to £777 by the time of his departure.[133]

Condon left Hamilton in May 1859 to establish a new mission at Greenock.[134] His replacement as mission priest was another Irish clergyman of outstanding abilities – James Danaher. Danaher remained at Hamilton until his death in 1886.[135]

It would not be an exaggeration to state that Condon helped save the Hamilton Mission from ruin. When he arrived at St Mary's in 1850 he found a mission which was in considerable difficulty: it had no funds, it was burdened with a heavy debt, and the congregation, through neglect, had become apathetic towards their religious duties. Condon's activities, particularly in the years in which he laboured alone, helped change this. Through his untiring and selfless efforts the mission went from strength to strength. A school was established, stations were opened at Strathaven and Cleland, the church was furnished, the finances were put in order, and, most importantly, the debt on St Mary's was significantly reduced. It should not be forgotten, however, that his efforts would have come to nothing had it not been for the commitment of his congregation, which was composed mainly of poor Irish immigrants. The dedication of both ensured that the Hamilton Mission recovered from the disasters of the 1840s.

References

1. James Darragh, 'The Catholic Population of Scotland since the year 1680', *Innes Review*, IV (1953), pp. 49–59; Christine Johnson, *Developments in the Roman Catholic Church in Scotland, 1789–1829* (Edinburgh, 1983), introduction, chapters 2, 17, 18; Christine Johnson, 'Secular Clergy of the Lowland District 1732–1829', *Innes Review*, XXXIV (1983), pp. 79–86; Bernard J Canning, *Irish-Born Secular Priests in Scotland 1829–1979* (Inverness, 1979), p. xxii; Alexander MacWilliam, 'The Glasgow Mission, 1792–1799', *Innes Review*, IV (1953), pp. 84–91; Parliamentary Papers, 1836 (40), XXIV, *Report on the State of the Irish Poor in Great Britain*, pp. 154–55.

2. For Irish Immigration during this period see James Edmund Handley,

The Irish in Scotland, 1798–1845 (Cork, 1943). The 1841 census shows that there were 126,321 people of Irish birth resident in Scotland. Of this total, 99,030, or just under 80 per cent, lived in the western lowland counties of Lanarkshire, Renfrewshire, Ayrshire, Dumbartonshire and Wigtonshire. These figures, of course, do not include those born in Scotland of Irish parents. Most of the immigrants came from the nine counties of Ulster, and a large number were Protestants.

3. For developments in the Catholic Church in the west of Scotland during the first half of the nineteenth century see Johnson, *Developments*, relevant chapters; Johnson, 'Secular Clergy', pp. 79–86; Christine Johnson, 'Scottish Secular Clergy, 1830–1878: The Western District'. *Innes Review*, XL (1989), pp. 106–152; Bernard Aspinwall, 'The Formation of the Catholic Community in the west of Scotland: Some Preliminary Outlines', *Innes Review*, XXXIII (1982), pp. 44–57; Bernard Aspinwall, 'Children of the Dead End: the Formation of the Modern Archdiocese of Glasgow, 1815–1914', *Innes Review*, XLIII (1992), pp. 119–144; John F McCaffrey, 'The Stewardship of Resources: Financial Strategies of Roman Catholics in the Glasgow District, 1800–70', in W J Sheils and Diana Wood (eds.), *Studies in Church History* volume 24: *The Church and Wealth* (Oxford, 1987), pp. 359–70; James McGloin, 'Catholic Education in Ayr, 1823–1918, part one', *Innes Review*, xiii (1962), pp. 77–90. See also the *Scottish Catholic Directories* from 1831–1851.

4. *Parliamentary Papers, 1837–1838, Reports of the Commissioners of Religious Instruction, Scotland, Second Report*, Appendix III, p. 275.

5. McGloin, 'Catholic Education', pp. 44–87; Johnson, 'Secular Clergy', p. 80.

6. *Report on the State of the Irish Poor*, p. 131; *Eighth Report of the Commissioners of Religious Instruction*, Appendix No. 1, p. 208.

7. *Ibid.*, p. 146; *Seventh Report of the Commissioners of Religious Instruction*, Appendix, p. 452.

8. *Ibid.*, p. 139; *Eighth Report of the Commissioners of Religious Instruction*, Appendix 1, p. 316; *Scottish Catholic Directory*, 1835, p. 48; 1838, p. 58.

9. The *Scottish Catholic Directories* from 1832 to 1836 state that the number of Catholics who formed the congregation at Dumbarton was 'from 450 to 500'. However, the Commissioners of Religious Instruction, who visited the town in August 1837 were informed by its priest that the number of Catholics under his charge totalled 1400. *Scottish Catholic Directory*, 1832, p. 58; 1834, p. 59; 1835, p. 48; 1836, p. 53; *Eighth Report of the Commissioners of Religious Instruction*, Appendix 1, p. 376.

10. *Report on the State of the Irish Poor*, p. 151; *Scottish Catholic Directory*, 1832, p. 57.

11. From 1731 until 1828 the Scottish Catholic Church was divided into two Districts, the Highland and the Lowland. In 1828 it was divided into three: the Eastern, Northern and Western. The last District contained the western lowland counties of Lanarkshire, Renfrewshire, Ayrshire, Dumbartonshire and Wigtonshire, as well as Argyllshire, Bute, Arran, the Western Islands and the southern part of Inverness-shire. Johnson, *Developments*, chapters 5, 27. *Scottish Catholic Directory*, 1831, p. 66.

12. *Second Report of the Commissioners of Religious Instruction*, Appendix III, pp. 275, 277.

13. *Eighth Report of the Commissioners of Religious Instruction*, Appendix I, pp. 208–9; *Scottish Catholic Directory*, 1831, p. 68.

14. *Seventh Report of the Commissioners of Religious Instruction*, Appendix, pp. 452, 455; *Report on the State of the Irish Poor*, p. 146.

15. *Eighth Report of the Commissioners of Religious Instruction*, Appendix I, p. 316.

16. *Report on the State of the Irish Poor*, p. 151; *Scottish Catholic Directory*, 1832, p. 57.

17. *Scottish Catholic Directory*, 1836, p. 52; *Seventh Report of the Commissioners of Religious Instruction*, Appendix, pp. 418–19; 455.

18. *Ibid.*, p. 47.

19. See, for example, Glasgow Archdiocesan Archives, Condon Diaries, Hamilton 1850–1859 [hereafter cited as Condon Diaries (Hamilton)], p. 97.

20. *Eighth Report of the Commissioners of Religious Instruction*, Appendix I, p. 211.

21. *Ibid.*, p. 211.

22. *Scottish Catholic Directory*, 1831, pp. 68, 70.

23. *Ibid.*, 1831, pp. 67, 69.

24. McCaffrey, 'Stewardship of Resources', pp. 364–65; Eighth Report of the Commissioners of Religious Instruction, Appendix I, pp. 210–11.

25. *Scottish Catholic Directory*, 1831, pp. 68, 70; 1832, p. 58.

26. *Ibid.*, 1831, pp. 67, 69; 1832, p. 58. See also Handley, *Irish in Scotland*, chapters 6, 7.

27. By 1831 the Glasgow priests had been able to establish only one Catholic school in the city without the aid of the Catholic Schools Society. *Ibid.*, 1831, p. 67; Handley, *op. cit.*, pp. 260–61. For Catholic education in nineteenth century Scotland see Handley, *op. cit.*, p. 260–62; James Handley, *The Irish in Modern Scotland* (Cork, 1947), chapter 7; Johnson, *Developments*, chapter 25; Thomas A Fitzpatrick, 'Catholic Education in Glasgow, Lanarkshire and South-West Scotland before 1872', *Innes Review*, XXXVI, 1985, pp. 86–96; *Catholic Secondary Education in South-West Scotland before 1972: Its Contribution to the change in status of the Catholic Community* (Aberdeen, 1986), chapter 3; Sister Martha Skinnider 'Catholic Elementary Education in Glasgow, 1818–1918' in T R Bone (ed.), *Studies in the History of Scottish Education, 1872–1939* (London, 1967), pp. 13–25; McGloin, 'Catholic Education' pp. 77–90. See also the *Scottish Catholic Directory* from 1831 onwards.

28. *Ibid.*, 1831, p. 67.

29. *Ibid.*, 1832, pp. 55–6; 1834, p. 57; 1835, p. 45.

30. *Ibid.*, 1831, p. 68; Johnson, *Developments*, p. 273; Handley, *Irish in Scotland*, p. 261; *Report on the State of the Irish Poor*, p. 131.

31. *Ibid.*, 1835, p. 48; Johnson, *op. cit.*, p. 223–24.

32. McGloin, 'Catholic Education', pp. 87–88.

33. *Scottish Catholic Directory*, 1831, p. 69.

34. McGloin 'Catholic Education' p. 88.

35. This account of the development of the Catholic Church in the western lowland counties is taken from information in the reports of the Western District contained in the *Scottish Catholic Directories* from 1831 to 1850. John Murdoch became a bishop and Andrew Scott's coadjutor in October 1833. When Scott died in October 1846, Murdoch succeeded him as Vicar Apostolic

of the Western District. Alexander Smith was consecrated Bishop and Co-adjutur to Murdoch in 1847.

36. *Ibid.*, 1867, pp. 140–41.

37. *Ibid.*, 1873, pp. 153–54.

38. This total is derived from Christine Johnson, 'Scottish Secular Clergy', pp. 110–40.

39. For the expansion of the coal and iron industries in Lanarkshire and Ayrshire from the mid-1830s, and the employment in them of Irish immigrants see Handley, *op. cit.*, pp. 90–91, 109–112; Alan B Campbell, *The Lanarkshire Miners. A Social History of their Trade Unions, 1775–1874* (Edinburgh, 1979) *passim*; Gordon M Wilson, *Alexander McDonald, Leader of the Miners* (Aberdeen, 1982), chapter 2.

40. *Scottish Catholic Directory*, 1848, pp. 73–4.

41. *Ibid.*, 1846, p. 72.

42. *Ibid.*, 1834, p. 58; 1839, p. 38.

43. Handley, *op. cit.*, p. 110.

44. *Scottish Catholic Directory*, 1846, p. 70.

45. *Ibid.*, 1850, p. 82. The other missions established in the western lowland counties during this period were Duntocher (1843), Stranraer (1845), and Port Glasgow (1846).

46. Condon Diaries (Hamilton) p. 13; *Scottish Catholic Directory*, 1845, p. 79.

47. The earliest reference in the Scottish Catholic Archives (hereafter SCA) to Glasgow priests saying Mass in Hamilton is in a letter from one of them, John Murdoch to a colleague John Forbes, dated February 1827. A letter from another of the Glasgow priests Andrew Scott that same month to Bishop Kyle states that Scott is 'glad to find the Hamilton people coming on so well'. In a letter to Bishop Paterson in December 1830 Scott informs him that Mass had been said at Hamilton for nearly two years, which was clearly not the case. Given the evidence the choice of late 1826 as being when the Glasgow priests first began to say Mass appears most probable. This becomes even more so when it is realised that until 1826 Scott and Murdoch were the only priests stationed at Glasgow and would probably not have the time to make regular visits to say Mass outside of the city. In 1826 two more priests came to the Glasgow Mission, and this probably enabled the clergy to begin saying Mass in Hamilton. SCA, Presholme letters, PL3/117/18 John Murdoch to John Forbes 19 February 1827; PL3/120/5 Andrew Scott to James Kyle, 26 February 1827; Blairs letters BL6/23/9 Andrew Scott to Alexander Paterson 8 December 1830; Christine Johnson, 'Secular Clergy', p. 83.

48. SCA, Presholme letters, PL3/117/8 John Murdoch to John Forbes 19 February 1827.

49. SCA, Blairs letters, BL6/23/9, Andrew Scott to Alexander Paterson, 8 December 1830.

50. *Ibid.*; Condon Dairies (Hamilton), p. 11; *The New Statistical Account of Scotland, vol. VI Lanark* (Edinburgh, 1835), p. 289.

51. See the *Scottish Catholic Directories from 1831 to 1839*.

52. *Ibid.*, 1837, p. 42; 1838, p. 56; 1839, pp. 38–39.

53. Condon Diaries (Hamilton), p. 18.

54. *Ibid.*, p. 11.

55. *Ibid.*, pp. 20–21. This evidence comes from an account of the parishes over which one of Scanlan's successors, James Smith (Mission priest 1846–50) had to minister to. There is no evidence to suggest that Scanlan's charge was any different from this.

56. SCA, Blairs letters BL6/483/7, Andrew Scott to James Kyle, 14 May 1845; BL6/483/10, Andrew Scott to Angus MacKenzie, 5 June 1845; BL6/479/13 John Murdoch to 'My Dear Lord' [Kyle] 19 June 1845; BL6/483/11 Andrew Scott to James Kyle 4 July 1845; *Condon Diaries (Hamilton)*, p. 13.

57. SCA, Blairs letters, BL6/483/11, Andrew Scott to James Kyle, 4 July 1845.

58. Condon Diaries (Hamilton), pp. 13–14; see also Canning, *Irish Born Secular Priests*, p. 349.

59. Canning, *Irish-born Priests*, p. 332.

60. Condon Diaries (Hamilton), pp. 16, 36.

61. *Scottish Catholic Directory*, 1846, p. 71.

62. Condon Diaries (Hamilton), p. 16.

63. *Ibid.*, p. 36. Here Condon states that the debt had been reduced to £1,600 by the time of Smith's arrival at Hamilton. However, this appears to be a mistake on his part, as on p. 67 he states that on 1 February 1851 Bishop Murdoch informed him that the debt of the Mission was '£1,600, viz. £100 more than when Mr Smith got charge of the Mission, a melancholy result'. Two years later Murdoch told Condon that the debt was almost £100 more than this figure, as Smith had not been honest in his accounts. Condon Diaries (Hamilton), pp. 200–1.

64. Johnson, 'Scottish Secular Clergy', p. 138.

65. *Scottish Catholic Directory*, 1849, p. 82.

66. Condon Diaries (Hamilton), p. 34.

67. *Ibid.*, pp. 11, 34; Canning, *Irish-born Clergy*, p. 26.

68. *Ibid.*, p. 20; *Scottish Catholic Directory*, 1849, p. 82.

69. SCA, Oban letters, OL2/78/10, John Murdoch, 'The Hamilton Mission' 31 May 1850 (letter of introduction for James Smith); Condon Diaries (Hamilton), p. 36.

70. Condon Diaries (Hamilton), p. 36.

71. *Ibid.*, pp. 5–6, 36, 37. Smith left to collect in Kilmarnock on 20 May 8 and returned to Hamilton nine days later. He made another trip between 6 June and 17 June. On 19 June he left Hamilton for England, and returned on 9 November.

72. *Ibid.*, p. 6.

73. *Ibid.*, p. 37.

74. *Ibid.*, pp. 37, 39.

75. *Ibid.*, p. 40.

76. *Ibid.*, p. 57.

77. Bernard Aspinwall, 'The Irish Abroad: Michael Condon in Scotland, 1845–1878' in W J Sheils and Diana Wood (eds.) *Studies in Church History volume 25: The Churches, Ireland and the Irish* (Oxford, 1985), pp. 277–297; *Scottish Catholic Directory*, 1903, pp. 250–52; Canning, *op. cit.*, pp. 48–54.

78. Condon Diaries (Hamilton), p. 35.

79. *Ibid.*, p. 57.

80. *Ibid.*, p. 66.

81. *Ibid.*, p. 68.

82. *Ibid.*, p. 68.

83. *Ibid.*, pp. 69–70.

84. *Glasgow Free Press*, 20 November 1852, quoted in Handley, *op. cit.*, p. 126. Condon was possibly the author of this article, as his account of the Hamilton Mission gives a very similar description of his congregation. Condon Diaries (Hamilton), p. 162.

85. Condon Diaries (Hamilton), pp. 111–112; Canning, *Irish-born priests*, p. 50. Condon's workload was slightly reduced in September 1852 when his congregation at Kilbride was given to the recently established Rutherglen Mission. See Condon Diaries (Hamilton), p. 153; *Scottish Catholic Directory*, 1854, p. 89.

86. *Ibid.*, p. 73.

87. For Condon's visits to the sick between 1850 and 1853 see *Ibid.*, pp. 73–4, 111–12; 175–76.

88. *Ibid.*, p. 112.

89. *Ibid.*, p. 73.

90. *Scottish Catholic Directory*, 1855, p. 89; Condon Diaries (Hamilton) pp. 245, 250–51.

91. *Ibid.*, 1855, p. 89.

92. Condon Diaries (Hamilton), p. 247.

93. *Ibid.*, p. 258.

94. *Ibid.*, pp. 261–62.

95. *Ibid.*, p. 262.

96. By the end of 1848, there were thirty-four priests, including Bishops, serving in the western lowlands: five years later the number had risen to forty-six. During this period three new parishes were established in Glasgow: St Patrick's in Anderston, St Joseph's in Cowcaddens and St Mungo's in Townhead. Furthermore, Missions were established at Lanark, Pollockshaws, Rutherglen, Maryhill, Johnstone, Old Cumnock, Saltcoats and Girvan. Priests were, of course, stationed at all the above places. See *Scottish Catholic Directory*, 1849, pp. 80–85 and *Ibid.*, 1854, pp. 85–94.

97. Condon Diaries (Hamilton), p. 224.

98. *Ibid.*, p. 273; Canning, *op. cit.*, p. 312.

99. *Ibid.*, p. 270.

100. *Ibid.*, p. 267.

101. *Ibid.*, p. 275.

102. *Ibid.*, pp. 282, 303.

103. *Ibid.*, p. 309.

104. *Ibid.*, pp. 313–15, 328–330, 340–44. For other examples of O'Leary's unacceptable behaviour see *Ibid.*, pp. 283, 304–5.

105. Johnson, 'Scottish Secular Clergy', p. 132; Condon Diaries (Hamilton), p. 368.

106. Condon Diaries (Hamilton), pp. 470–71.

107. SCA, Blairs letters, BL7/40/20, Michael Condon, 'Memorial to the War Office' (copy); BL7/40/19 Michael Condon to P McLaughlan 20 January 1858; BL7/40/21 Michael Condon to P McLaughlan 2 February 1858; BL7/40/22 Michael Condon to P McLaughlan 16 June 1858. Condon Diaries (Hamilton), pp. 467–8.

108. Condon Diaries (Hamilton), p. 475.

109. *Ibid.*, p. 510.

110. *Glasgow Free Press*, 3 December 1859, quoted in Canning, *Irish-born priests*, p. 235.

111. Condon Diaries (Hamilton), pp. 74, 111, 175–76, 321–22, 383, 425, 465.

112. *Ibid.*, p. 459.

113. *Scottish Catholic Directory*, 1855, p. 89; Condon Diaries (Hamilton), pp. 162, 442.

114. Condon Diaries (Hamilton), p. 472.

115. *Ibid.*, pp. 225; *Scottish Catholic Directory*, 1855, p. 89; *Ibid.*, 1859, p. 100. Condon received his gig in early December 1853 but not his horse until a month later. In the intervening period he hired a horse. Condon's 1851 census showed that 206 out of the 2,200 members of his congregation lived in Strathaven, which was in the parish of Avondale; Condon Diaries (Hamilton), p. 68.

116. *Ibid.*, pp. 227, 249, 316–17. *Scottish Catholic Directory*, 1859, p. 100. Condon's 1851 census revealed that 392 out of the 2,200 members of his congregation resided at Cleland, which was in the parish of Shotts. No other town or village in the Hamilton Mission, apart from Hamilton itself, had a larger number of Roman Catholics.

117. *Ibid.*, p. 164.

118. *Ibid.*, p. 102.

119. *Ibid.*, p. 164. Fitzpatrick states that 'In 1852 the parochial school of St Mary's in Hamilton opened with a roll of sixty, under Sister Mary Phillipa . . .' Fitzpatrick 'Catholic Education in Glasgow, Lanarkshire and South-West Scotland', pp. 93–4. There is, however, no evidence whatsoever in the *Scottish Catholic Directories* of the period or in Condon's account of the Hamilton Mission, to support this assertion.

120. *Ibid.*, p. 165.

121. *Ibid.*, p. 215.

122. *Ibid.*, p. 197.

123. *Ibid.*, p. 178; *Scottish Catholic Directory*, 1855, pp. 89–90; 1859, p. 100. The annual donation of the Duchess continued until at least 1862.

124. *Ibid.*, p. 197; *Scottish Catholic Directory*, 1855, p. 89; 1859, p. 100.

125. *Scottish Catholic Directory*, 1855, p. 89; 1859, p. 100; Condon Diaries (Hamilton), p. 40.

126. Condon Diaries (Hamilton), pp. 204, 364, 370, 474; *Scottish Catholic Directory*, 1855, p. 89.

127. *Ibid.*, pp. 365, 372, 419, 428, 448; *Scottish Catholic Directory*, 1857, p. 108.

128. *Ibid.*, pp. 154, 193–4.

129. *Ibid.*, pp. 204, 364, 365, 396, 397, 398, 418.

130. *Ibid.*, pp. 56, 60, 87, 123.

131. This can be established by an examination of the income and expenditure of the Hamilton Mission, the figures for which can be found in the Condon Diaries (Hamilton).

132. *Ibid.*, pp. 104, 494.

133. *Ibid.*, p. 513.

134. *Ibid.*, pp. 503–4, 508, 511.

135. Canning, *Irish-born priests*, pp. 71–74.

CHAPTER 2

The Catholic Community in Hamilton, c.1800–1914[1]

Martin J. Mitchell

PART 1

The report for Hamilton in *The Statistical Account of Scotland*, compiled in the 1790s, reveals that there were not any Roman Catholics then resident in the civil parish.[2] In the *New Statistical Account* the report on Hamilton, dated July 1835, states that the number of Catholic families in the parish was forty-five.[3] A census taken some months prior to this report calculated the population of Hamilton to be 9,822.[4] Although the *New Statistical Account* provides no further information on these families, they were undoubtedly part of the influx of Irish immigrants to the west of Scotland over the previous four decades.[5] It is not known when these Irish Catholics arrived in Hamilton, but a number were present by the mid-1820s, when the priests from Glasgow began saying mass in the town at regular intervals.[6]

The largest occupational group in Hamilton during the first half of the nineteenth century was the handloom weavers.[7] It is probable that a number of the Irish Catholics in the parish in 1835 were also employed in weaving, as this was a trade which attracted many of the Irish workers in the west of Scotland during the pre-famine era of immigration.[8] Some of the other Catholic workers in Hamilton in 1835 were probably among the 252 labourers recorded in the parish at the time,[9] as labouring was another occupation in which many Irish immigrants were found during this period.[10]

It is not until the 1850s that more information is available on the size and occupational structure of the Catholic population of Hamilton. As the previous chapter has shown, in 1851 the priest in charge of the Hamilton Mission, Michael Condon, took a census of his congregation, who were scattered over eleven civil parishes in the Middle Ward of Lanarkshire. He found that in Hamilton the number of Catholics was 746.[11] The national census of Scotland for that year recorded a total of 11,740 persons resident in the parish.[12] Condon's second census, taken in 1857, shows that the number of Catholics in Hamilton had risen to 1,411.[13] The table below gives a break down of Condon's figures for both years:

Table 1.

Year	Hamilton	Motherwell	Quarter	M. Yarnock	Total
1851	702	30	14	0	746
1857	1022	300	74	15	1411

With regard to occupations, the *Glasgow Free Press* of November 1852 states, of the Catholics in Hamilton, that 'whilst a few live as brokers, the great majority support life by vending delph, fish, whiting, or exchanging them to the country people for rags, bones, old iron, etc.'[14] This description, however, almost certainly applies only to the town of Hamilton and its immediate vicinity. The above table shows that fourteen Catholics lived in Quarter, which was a mining village about four miles south of the town of Hamilton.[15] In Motherwell, most of the Irish workers at this time were railway labourers.[16]

The massive increase in the number of Catholics in and around the town of Hamilton, and at Quarter, between 1851 and 1857, was almost certainly caused by the growth of coalmining in these areas. The 1850s was the decade which saw the beginning of the expansion of the mining industry in Hamilton, a development which attracted many newcomers to the parish, including Irish workers and their families.[17]

The increase in Condon's congregation at Motherwell appears to have been the result of many Irish workers entering the district to form part of the labour force at the Malleable Iron Works, which re-opened in 1853.[18] By 1861 there were 540 people of Irish birth resident in Motherwell, and most of the workers among them were employed in the iron works.[19] Although part of Motherwell was in the parish of Hamilton,[20] the Malleable Iron Works and the houses in which its workers lived were in the parish of Dalziel,[21] and so it would appear that Condon erred in including a figure of 300 for Motherwell in his enumeration of the Hamilton parish. Furthermore, it is worth noting that in both his censuses Condon does not provide any figures for Motherwell in his accounts for the parish of Dalziel, which suggests that he was simply unaware of the parochial location of the district of Motherwell in which his congregation resided.

During the period 1857 to 1914 the Catholic population of Hamilton continued to rise. This was not solely due to the natural growth of the number of Catholics, but was also the result of Irish workers and families continuing to enter the parish to work in the mines.[22] By the early 1900s Catholic Poles and Lithuanians were also employed in the pits, particularly in the Burnbank district.[23] It would appear that from the middle of the nineteenth century until the outbreak of the First World War, most Catholic workers in Hamilton were employed in the mining industry.[24] It was not only Catholics who worked in the mines: the *Third Statistical Account of Scotland* states that 'the vast majority of Hamiltonians, at the beginning of the present century and for a considerable time afterwards, lived on wages earned in the pits, or were largely dependent on the prosperity of the coal industry'.[25]

It is, unfortunately, impossible to establish the exact size of the Catholic population of Hamilton over this period. The first annual return which is available for the Hamilton Mission is for the year ending 1869, and the number of the congregation is given as 1,870.[26] However, although the geographical and numerical extent of the mission had been greatly reduced since 1857 by the establishment of missions at Strathaven, Chapelhall, and Wishaw,[27] the congregation of the Hamilton Mission in 1869 still included a number who resided outwith the civil parish of Hamilton. These were the Catholics of Blantyre, and of the part of Motherwell which was in the parish of Dalziel.[28] Furthermore, the Catholics in and around Quarter, and those in Larkhall (part of which was in the parish of Hamilton) were members of the congregation of the Strathaven Mission.[29]

A mission was founded at Motherwell in 1873, and one at Blantyre in 1877.[30] With the establishment of the latter it would appear that Hamilton Mission no longer had any members of its congregation who lived outside the boundaries of the civil parish of Hamilton.[31] Its annual return for the year ending 1877 calculated the number of Catholics at around 1,500.[32] The Catholics who lived in and around Quarter, and those in the 'Hamilton' part of Larkhall were, however, still not part of the Hamilton Mission.[33] Also, it is probable that the Catholics resident in the area of Motherwell which was in the parish of Hamilton, had become members of the congregation of the recently established Motherwell Mission.

By the end of 1882 the congregation of the Hamilton Mission had risen to around 1,900.[34] The following July the Cadzow Mission was opened. Its chapel-school, dedicated to Our Lady and St Anne, was consecrated and formally opened in September 1883. The mission was located about halfway between Quarter and Cadzow, and its congregation was composed of the Catholics living in the mining districts of Quarter, Mid-Quarter, Low Quarter, Eddlewood, and Low Waters.[35] Indeed, the *Glasgow Observer*, the newspaper for the Irish Catholics of the west of Scotland, stated in 1897 that the Catholics of the mission were 'entirely of the mining class'.[36] The size of the congregation when the mission was established is not known, but by the end of 1884 its number was calculated to be 1,020.[37]

With the establishment of the Cadzow Mission the number of Catholics attached to the Hamilton Mission whose chapel was, of course, St Mary's, was reduced to around 1,300 by the end of 1883.[38] Nine years later, however, the number had dramatically increased to an estimated 2,700.[39] (The congregation of the Cadzow Mission numbered 1,250 at this time.[40]) As a result of its increasing population, the Hamilton Mission was divided and a new mission was opened in Burnbank in 1893. Its chapel, dedicated to St Cuthbert, was opened on 1 October of that year.[41] In the first annual return of the new mission, the number of the congregation is recorded as 1,045,[42] The overwhelming majority of Catholics in Burnbank at this time, and in the years leading up to the outbreak of the Great War, were also employed in the mining industry.[43]

At the end of 1892, some months prior to the establishment of the Burnbank Mission, the Catholic population of the Hamilton and Cadzow Missions combined was 3,950.[44] From 1893 until 1914 congregational statistics for all three missions in Hamilton are available for only six of the years in this period. These are shown in the table below, along with the population of the parish of Hamilton recorded in the national censuses of 1901 and 1911. The annual returns for the missions were compiled at the end of each year for which they were applicable and were sent to the Archdiocese the following January. The national census for 1901 was taken on 31 March, and for 1911 on 2 April.

Table 2.

Year	Hamilton (St Mary's)	Cadzow (Our Lady & St Anne's)	Burnbank (St Cuthbert's)	Total Pop. of the 3 Missions	Population of the Parish of Hamilton
1900	2,700	1,400	1,230	5,330	
1901					40,372
1906	3,750	1,600	1,950	7,300	
1908	3,800	1,650	2,010	7,460	
1909	3,900	1,635	2,050	7,585	
1910	4,000	1,707	2,500	8,207	
1911					46,419
1912	4,250	1,760	2,240	8,250	

Sources: G.A.A., Annual Returns: MW19, Hamilton Mission, 1900, 1906, 1908–10, 1912; MW8, Cadzow Mission, 1900, 1906, 1908–10, 1912; MW7, Burnbank Mission, 1900, 1906, 1908–10, 1912. *Census of Scotland*,

As a result of boundary charges, by the time of the 1901 census parts of the towns of Larkhall and Motherwell were no longer in the civil parish of Hamilton.[45] It must be emphasised, however, that the above combined totals of the three missions do not necessarily equal the actual number of Catholics in Hamilton. It may have been the case that any Catholics who lived to the south or east of Quarter attended the nearby church of St Mary's in

Larkhall, as opposed to the more distant Our Lady and St Anne's in Cadzow.

The Catholic community in Hamilton in the period covered by this chapter was, like all other Catholic communities in Scotland, overwhelmingly working class in its composition. In a number of areas in the west of the country, however, there were small groups of Catholic businessmen and professionals, and this was also the situation in Hamilton, certainly from the 1870s onwards.[46] For example, James Carragher was a draper whose business was in the town's Quarry Street;[47] Robert Slorach was a solicitor who became one of the Sheriff-Clerk Deputies of Lanarkshire – he settled in the parish in 1884 after being promoted to the Hamilton District;[48] James Haley was the agent for the British Linen Bank in the town, and his son Francis was a sub-agent in the same company's office in Glasgow.[49] William Meechan was a former miner who became a publican.[50] Another Catholic publican in the town was John H. McLaughlin. He was one of the founders of Glasgow Celtic F.C., and in the club's early years was its secretary and representative to the Scottish Football Association. McLaughlin was one of the leading figures in the development of Scottish football during the 1890s. He also played a major role in Celtic becoming a limited liability company in 1897, whereupon he became one of the company's first directors. McLaughlin was then elected first Chairman of the club, and remained so until his death in 1909. During these years he was also, for a period, President of the Scottish Football Association.[51] Another early shareholder in Celtic was Thomas Moore, of 97 Quarry Street, Hamilton. He had 100 shares in 1897, although his occupation is not given in the list of shareholders.[52]

As was the case with a number of the missions in the west of Scotland,[53] those in Hamilton borrowed money from some of the more prosperous members of their congregations. In 1878, James Danaher, the priest in charge of the Hamilton Mission from 1859 to 1886, borrowed £400 from John Warren, a spirit merchant in the town. In 1880 he borrowed £400 from Joseph Small, and two years later £500 from Patrick Small. These sums were used to fund the building of additions to the school.[54] Patrick Small also loaned £200 to the Cadzow Mission in 1885.[55] Joseph Lynas, a pawnbroker in Burnbank,[56] made several loans to the missions during the late nineteenth and early twentieth centuries: to the Hamilton Mission (St Mary's) he advanced £140 in 1885, £500 in 1906, and £800 in 1911; the Cadzow Mission (Our Lady and St Anne's) borrowed £1,000 from him in 1885, and the Burnbank Mission (St Cuthbert's) £300 in 1894.[57] The sums loaned by these individuals were considerable for the time: in 1877, for example, the *Hamilton Advertiser* stated that the average wage for Scottish miners was four shillings a day; by 1912 their wage rate was six shillings a day.[58]

PART 2

From 1843, when the Hamilton Mission was founded, until 1914, a number of institutions and societies were established both for and by the Catholic community. From the Church's viewpoint the schools were the most essential of these. Catholic education in Hamilton in the years to 1859 has been discussed in the previous chapter, and the subsequent period will be examined in Chapter 3. After the schools, temperance societies were arguably the most important of the organisations formed for Catholic communities during this period – certainly from the standpoint of the clergy. In Hamilton, a temperance society was established for its Catholics even before the opening of the mission. In 1840, one of the priests at Glasgow, James Enraght, formed a temperance organisation in the city. By the following March he had founded a number of branch societies, including one in Hamilton.[59] It is not known for how long it lasted. When Michael Condon took charge of the mission one of his first acts was to initiate a temperance society for youngsters. He enrolled eighty-eight members to begin with and seventy more within two weeks.[60] During James Danaher's period in charge of St Mary's (1859–86) a Catholic Total Abstinence Society was formed.[61] This was replaced in 1889 by a branch of the Church's own temperance organisation, the League of the Cross.[62] Branches of the society were also established at Our Lady and St Anne's in 1887, and at St Cuthbert's in 1893.[63]

37

As the Catholic Total Abstinence Society and the League of the Cross were Church organisations, the clergy at Hamilton were naturally very active in them. They presided at meetings and administered the pledge to new members.[64] The priests believed that alcohol was the cause of a number of social and moral problems. Peter Donnelly, in charge of the Hamilton Mission from 1886 until his death in 1902, told a large meeting of Catholics in the Town Hall in October 1890 that in his experience:

> If a man were a total abstainer he had nothing to find fault with in him. If they were to enquire of the Sheriffs and Magistrates they would find that the crime of the country was almost entirely due to the curse of drink.[65]

A year later, at the second annual reunion of the Hamilton (i.e. the St Mary's) branch of the League of the Cross, Donnelly informed his audience that he 'had to acknowledge that in going over the parish he found the houses of the Leaguers homes of prosperity, peace and happiness'.[66]

The League of the Cross was not a society exclusively for men. By October 1890, one hundred out of the four hundred members of the Hamilton branch were women.[67] In February 1913 a branch of the women's League of the Cross was established at St Mary's.[68] This does not necessarily mean, however, that a number of the female Catholic population of Hamilton had a drink problem! For example, at the second annual meeting of the Hamilton branch of the League, one of the speakers was Father Hughes of Cleland. He told his audience that:

> The League of the Cross was a religious institution, and he had to say that, no matter how the men might labour, that no matter how successful their efforts might be, their work would not be permanent unless their mothers, daughters, and sisters joined them in this holy crusade . . . The Church appealed to them now to save Catholic society, and through saving Catholic society save society in general by joining the League of the Cross . . ., they would not be asked to become preachers or appear on platforms. No; their influence and council was wanted in the house, at the christening, at the wedding, and at the wake. (Loud cheers.) As Christian women he asked them,

was it right that infants should be welcomed into the world by a shower-bath of whisky. (Renewed cheering.) They could keep whisky out of their households and if drunken men brought it in they should break the bottles. (Cheers.) He believed that much of the domestic misery that existed was due to the whisky bottle, and if a young woman refused to take the glass of wine and say that they would have nothing to do with the young man who touched it, a reformation would be wrought in the habits of Catholic society.[69]

Similarly, the concern of the St Mary's branch at this time for children and temperance,[70] along with Condon's earlier Juvenile Temperance Society, should be viewed as attempts by the clergy to educate the young as to their perceived view of the dangers of alcohol, and should not be regarded as evidence of a drink problem among the Catholic children of Hamilton.

Although Donnelly was a strong advocate of total abstinence it would appear that he experienced difficulty in persuading a number of his congregation to join the League of the Cross. In October 1891, he told the second annual reunion of the St Mary's branch, which at that time numbered around 700, that:

> the League since its inception had made great improvements on many people in the parish. It had changed many from a wicked to a good life. However, it did not come up to his expectations. It had not gathered into the ranks all those who were drinking to such an extent that they were unworthy of the name Christian. It was true that the League had accomplished a great deal, but it still had a large field before it.[71]

There was also the problem of leakage. In January 1892 Donnelly remarked that 'a great many had broken away during the holidays'.[72] Three months later the president of the branch, James MacHale, stated in his annual report that although progress had been steady, 'the falling off at times was distressing . . .'.[73] Despite this Donnelly was 'well pleased' with the condition of the branch.[74] Indeed, in March 1892 he told his congregation that all their societies were flourishing, especially the League of the Cross.[75]

In order to further the cause of temperance Donnelly decided to build a large hall for his congregation at St Mary's. It was erected next to the school and was opened on 23 December 1892.

Prior to the start of the concert held to celebrate the event Donnelly explained to his audience why he felt that the hall was essential for them:

> ... there was a great need for some places where men could go after work for rational and harmless amusement. Under present conditions the only place available was the public house, and the evils arising from making it a resort were well known. To counteract this temptation, and provide a hall where his people might meet socially, the hall in which they were in had been built. He did not know whether it was altogether prudent to proceed with an undertaking such as this with only a small portion of the money in hand, but his anxiety to provide healthy entertainment for his people had induced him to go on with it and trust to the Catholics of Hamilton to support him in paying off the cost.

The hall had seating for 500 people and cost £1,150 to build.[76]

The St Mary's branch of the League of the Cross was still active in Hamilton in 1914. There is some evidence which suggests that it may have experienced a period of stagnation or even decline in the late 1900s, if not earlier. In January 1911 the *Glasgow Observer* thought it worthy of note that since it had been reorganised, the St Mary's branch had 'been making wonderful progress, every meeting seeing quite large numbers of new names being added to the roll. The meetings are being held now on Sunday evenings in the schools, and on every occasion they are attended by large numbers of the members of the parish'.[77] A year later the paper reported that the League was 'making rapid progress in Hamilton parish'.[78] Meetings of the branch in 1911 and 1912 attracted large attendances.[79]

Peter Donnelly's reason for erecting a Church hall in 1892 was to provide his congregation with a place other than the public house where they could meet and relax after work. The St Mary's branch of the League of the Cross, and its predecessor, the Catholic Total Abstinence Society, also worked unceasingly to provide alternative attractions to the drink-based culture of the time. They held lectures, concerts, and socials[80] and organised excursions, as occurred in July 1892 when the branch had its fourth annual outing, on this occasion to Stirling. The day's events included races, football matches, dances, and sightseeing.[81] The branches of the League at Our Lady and St Anne's, and at St Cuthbert's, also held these types of events.[82]

Two other important church organisations in Hamilton in these years were the St Vincent de Paul Society, which assisted poor members of the congregation, and the Christian Doctrine Society. The latter, established at St Mary's in 1880,[83] was composed of the Sunday-school teachers, and its principal aims were 'the promotion of Catholic doctrine, and the consideration of such means as are best calculated to induce the children to turn out on Sundays, not only to Mass, but to Sunday school'.[84] Pupils with good attendance received prizes, such as copies of the Bible, prayer books, and rosaries.[85] The organisation is included in the list of societies for St Mary's in the *Scottish Catholic Directory* until the edition for 1892. Thereafter there is no mention of it. A branch of the St Vincent de Paul Society was established at St Mary's in 1853. It appears that it lapsed in 1887 and was not re-established until 1906.[86] As well as helping the needy the St Mary's branch held socials and organised concerts to raise funds.[87]

From the 1880s onwards, branches of the main Irish and Catholic benefit societies, such as the Irish National Foresters, the Ancient Order of Hibernians, and the Catholic Insurance Society, were established in Hamilton. These branches, like those of the church organisations, also had a social function: they too held concerts, soirées, excursions, and demonstrations.[88]

There is evidence that, as well as having problems with its church societies, St Mary's also experienced occasional falls in attendance at mass. This occurred during James Smith's period in charge of the Hamilton Mission (1846–50), although, as the Chapter 1 has shown, the situation appears to have been one of his own making. During Peter Donnelly's time at St Mary's the same problem arose, as the following report from the *Glasgow Observer* of 28 September 1895 makes clear:

> The Rev. Father Donnelly on Sunday last delivered an earnest exhortation on the duty of observing Sunday as a day of holiness. He deplored the great laxity of Catholics in attending Mass. They had every inducement to attend Divine service, but they were callous in the extreme. If all the Catholics in Hamilton attended Mass as

they should do their Church, large as it was, would not be capable of accommodating them. Those who were callous in attending the services of the Church were, of course, similarly indifferent in their support of the Church. For their own sakes particularly, he appealed to them to remember that neglect of their duty to their Church here, would inevitably be punished hereafter.

In this address Donnelly alludes to a reduction in the income of St Mary's as a result of the drop in attendance. This appears to have been a problem around this time. The previous May, the *Glasgow Observer* reported that Donnelly, clearly a formidable figure, published each Sunday the names of those of his congregation who were defaulting in their contributions to the Church.[89] It is not known whether the problems Donnelly faced in 1895 were solved in subsequent years, or existed at St Cuthbert's and Our Lady and at St Anne's.

PART 3

Problems of a different kind occurred for the Catholic church in Hamilton from the 1890s onwards, with the arrival in the parish of Lithuanian and Polish Catholics. The male workers among them found employment in the mines.[90] These immigrants, like the Lithuanians and Poles in other mining areas in Lanarkshire, experienced difficulties in adjusting to their new environment. They came from a different background and culture from the members of Catholic communities in the areas where they settled, and they spoke a different language. Indeed, they probably experienced some hostility from them, as a number of Lithuanian and Polish miners entered the pits as strike-breakers. Others were employed as cheap labour. These issues greatly concerned miners in the west of Scotland at this time. There was also the fear that, as these new workers were unskilled, they were a threat to safety in the mines.[91]

Before discussing these immigrants and the Catholic Church in Hamilton, an important point must be made. Sometimes these immigrants are described in the press, or in other sources, solely as Poles; at other times, only as Lithuanians. According to the historian who has examined the responses to these immigrants in the Lanarkshire coalfield, the majority of them were Lithuanians.[92]

A few years after they first arrived in the Lanarkshire coalfield, the Lithuanians and Poles began agitating for their own churches and priests. In 1903 Archbishop John Maguire informed them that their request could not be granted, but soon afterwards allowed a Lithuanian priest to minister in the county. The *Glasgow Observer* in November 1905 reported that this priest had returned home the previous August, 'and since then the aliens have been handicapped in the proper exercise of their religious duties, owing to the difficulty experienced in making themselves understood'. As a result, demands for a separate parish for the immigrants revived, and a number of meetings were held that autumn in areas where the Poles and Lithuanians had settled.[93]

One such meeting was held by the Poles and Lithuanians resident in Burnbank. It took place in the Masonic Hall on 2 November 1905, and was attended by over five hundred of the immigrants. The *Glasgow Observer* reported that:

> The chairman stated that a communication had been addressed to the Archbishop of Glasgow, inquiring upon what conditions a native priest would be allowed to labour among his brethren in this country. The Archbishop's reply, it was stated, was to the effect that the various chapels would be at the disposal of the people for the holding of services in their own language, but that no special mass could be said by the native priest: baptisms and marriages were to be celebrated by the native priest under the supervision of the parish priest.

The Archbishop's conditions did not meet with the approval of the meeting. The paper also reported that a petition to the Archbishop for a Lithuanian parish was currently being prepared.[94]

The following January, John Czuberkis, a Lithuanian priest, was placed at St Mary's. The *Glasgow Observer* stated that 'His time and energy will be devoted to ministering to the spiritual needs of his fellow countrymen, for whom Hamilton is now a centre'.[95] The following month Czuberkis held a special service at St Mary's for the Poles and Lithuanians, on the occasion of the

Feast of the Purification.[96] In April, he held another special service in the church, to celebrate Easter. Lithuanians and Poles from all over Lanarkshire, numbering nearly 1,500, attended. The *Glasgow Observer* reported that:

> The reverend gentleman preached to his fellow-countrymen in their native tongue, and after the sermon, which was appropriate to the joyous occasion, hymns in the Lithuanian language were introduced. The service lasted upwards of four hours, and a special feature of it was the congregational singing of the native hymns, set to beautiful music, and rendered with deep feeling and powerful effect.

Czuberkis was one of two Lithuanian priests active in the country at this time, and the paper concluded its report by stating that 'for religious purposes the Lithuanians are now thoroughly organised'.[97]

Czuberkis left Hamilton the following year.[98] There is not much information concerning the Poles and Lithuanians in the parish in the *Glasgow Observer* from 1906 to 1914. It would appear, however, that they continued to act as a group and remained relatively isolated from Hamilton's Irish Catholic community. For example, in January 1912 around four hundred of them held their own social and dance at St Cuthbert's, presided over by Father Duncan Brown. The music was performed by their own band.[99] In March, the same number of Lithuanians and Poles 'approached their Easter Duty' at St Cuthbert's.[100]

By 1914 it is possible that relations between the Irish Catholic community and the Polish/Lithuanian Catholic community had improved. During the miners' general strike of 1912, a number of the Polish and Lithuanian miners in Lanarkshire also struck work,[101] and it would appear that in Hamilton they joined in the stoppage along with the Catholic miners and the native Scottish miners (see below).

Part 4

The principal political issue for Irish Catholic communities in Great Britain during the period 1850–1914 was the condition of Ireland. In 1870 the Home Rule Movement was founded in

Dublin, with the establishment of the Home Government Association. Its aim was to campaign for the repeal of the 1800 Act of the Union of Ireland and Great Britain, and the establishment of a parliament in Dublin which would deal with Irish domestic issues. Branches of the society were soon founded in England and Scotland. Over subsequent decades the movement went through several changes of name; for example, the Irish Land League, the Irish National League, and the United Irish League.

The main purpose of the branches from the early 1880s onwards, when the Irish National Movement was known as the Irish National League, was to mobilise the role of the Irish communities in general elections behind candidates endorsed by the executive of that body. In 1885 it ordered the branches to vote for the Tories in order to demonstrate to the Liberal Party, the ally of the Irish Parliamentary Party, that it could not automatically depend on the support of the Irish Nationalist electorate in Great Britain. In subsequent elections in Scotland the executive usually endorsed candidates of the Liberal Party, which introduced home rule bills in 1886, 1892, and 1912. There were some occasions, however, when Liberal candidates who were regarded as lukewarm to home rule did not receive the endorsement of the executive. When this occurred, Irish nationalist voters abstained, or voted for labour candidates, or, on one occasion, actually supported the Tory candidate, whose party was implacably opposed to home rule. This happened in 1900, in the Blackfriers Hutchesontown constituency of Glasgow. There is also evidence of local branches and Irish electors voting against the wishes of the executive.[102]

As the overwhelming majority of Catholics in Hamilton at this period were either Irish or of Irish descent, it is not surprising that a branch of the organisation which directed the home rule movement was established in Hamilton in the early 1870s.[103] By the late 1890s there were two other branches of the Irish National League in the parish, at Cadzow and at Burnbank.[104]

The parish of Hamilton was not a single parliamentary entity in these years. Between 1832 and 1918 the burghs of Hamilton, Airdrie, Lanark, Falkirk, and Linlithgow were grouped together in the one constituency, known as the Falkirk Burghs.[105] The part of the remaining area of the parish of Hamilton which lay south and west of the Clyde was, after the Redistribution Act of 1885, included in the constituency of Mid-Lanark, along with the parishes of Rutherglen, Carmunnock, Cambuslang, Blantyre, Dalserf, Cambusnethan, and part of the parish of Cathcart: the part of the country area of Hamilton which lay north and east of the Clyde formed part of the north-east Lanark constituency, which also included the parishes of New Monklands, Bothwell, Shotts, and Dalziel.[106]

In the parliamentary elections of 1885 the executive of the Irish National League instructed its branches to mobilise the Irish Nationalist vote for the Tory candidates. In subsequent general and by-elections in the constituencies of Mid-Lanarkshire and the Falkirk Burghs, it would appear that the executive decreed that the Irish Nationalist vote should go to the Liberal candidates. From the available evidence it seems that the branches in Hamilton loyally carried out these directives. For example, in early 1886, James MacHale, president of the Hamilton branch of the Irish National League, stated that in the election of 1885 the Irish votes of Hamilton 'had polled almost to a man in accordance with the directions of the League'.[107] In the General Election of 1886 the *Glasgow Observer* reported that the Liberal candidate for Mid-Lanark received the vote of the Irish nationalist electors in the Hamilton part of the constituency.[108] After the election of January 1910 the paper stated that in Hamilton:

> The result of the Falkirk Burghs election was received with great interest, and the Irish section of the community were quite jubilant when it became known that Mr. Murray Macdonald had won the seat by a substantial majority. The Nationalist electors polled to the last available man, and there can be no doubt but that the mandate of the Executive was loyally obeyed.[109]

In the election the following December, the Liberal, Murray Macdonald, was once again the candidate whom the executive of the United Irish League instructed the Irish Nationalists to vote for.[110]

There were attempts in Hamilton to persuade the Irish electors to vote and act in the interests of their class, as opposed to concerning themselves almost exclusively with the condition of Ireland. In January 1886 the *Glasgow Observer* published a letter from James Furie, an Irish miner resident in Burnbank, who was active in trade-union affairs. Furie believed that the time had come for workers in Scotland and England to send their own representatives to Parliament:

> As an Irishman, I fully admit, sympathise with and deeply regret the cruel wrongs that Ireland has suffered at the hands of the British Government. But have we, the working men of Scotland, not suffered from the same cause? . . . Labour, I see, has but an infinitesimal representation, when compared with capital, land, law, army, navy or the Church. Until such time as the toiling masses of both Scotland and England wake up to the fact that they are as able to send men of their own class to represent them in Parliament as the poor, downtrodden peasantry of Ireland, we will never be any better, with all our boasting about the franchise. If, therefore, we wish to be represented in Parliament we must pay for it. Ireland has never been represented until now. So if the poor Irish peasants can pay their members, I surely think we can do the same.

Furie suggested that a national fund be started for the payment of Labour representatives and he hoped that by the next election a few of them would be elected to Parliament.[111] Furie's letter did not, however, receive much support in the letter columns of the *Glasgow Observer*.[112]

An opportunity for Irish and Scottish working-class voters in Hamilton to make clear their views on this subject came two years later at the Mid-Lanark by-election. James Keir Hardie stood as a Labour candidate and appealed for Irish support. The executive of the Irish National League was hostile to Hardie's candidature and ordered its local branches in the constituency to support the Liberal candidate. The Irish vote remained loyal to the INL directive. The Liberal candidate was returned, and Hardie came bottom of the poll with only 617 votes; it is clear that he did not receive the support of even the majority of Scottish workers.[113] Hardie's failure to persuade Irish electors to vote for a labour programme does not necessarily mean that the Irish in Mid-Lanark were hostile to the principle of independent Labour representation. As the *Glasgow Observer* stated at the time of the by-election:

> We cannot afford, much as we would like to serve the interests of the workmen – if Mr. Hardie's return would be a gain to them, which we question – to throw in our lot with any new causes or new programmes. We want to settle Home Rule first.[114]

No doubt it was this argument which prevented Labour candidates from attracting the Irish vote away from the Liberal party at subsequent elections in the constituency.[115]

In the elections for the constituency of north-east Lanarkshire from 1886 onwards it would appear that the local branches were instructed to vote for the Liberal candidate in all but one of the contests.[116] This was in the by-election of 1901, when the Irish were directed to vote for the Labour candidate, as the Liberal was regarded as unsympathetic to Home Rule. It would appear, however, that on this occasion the wishes of the executive were not completely obeyed.[117] This was also the case in the by-election of 1904, when the Liberals put forward a new candidate who was acceptable to the executive of the United Irish League. A sizeable number of Irish Nationalist electors, however, voted for the Labour candidate. It is not known what proportion, if any, of the dissenting Irish vote on both occasions came from Hamilton.[118]

The branches in Hamilton of the various organisations which controlled the Home Rule movement over the 1871–1914 period were not just active at election times. Between these contests the branches held meetings and socials and gave financial contributions to their executive, as well as sending representatives to the annual convention.[119] The branches were also active in ensuring that all Irish nationalists who were eligible to vote were registered.[120] Meetings were held, whose purpose was to educate and inform. For example, speakers would lecture on Irish history or on the current state of politics in Ireland and Great Britain. Topics included 'The Irish Rebellion of 1798', 'Pauperism in Ireland', 'Ireland Past and Present', 'The Land War in Ireland', 'Poets and Poetry of Ireland', 'Current Politics', 'The Life and Times of Daniel O'Connell'.[121] Various Irish Nationalist MPs also visited

Hamilton to address the branches on the current political situation.[122]

Such activities were not, however, constant throughout this period, and the Irish National Movement in Hamilton occasionally experienced some considerable problems. In January 1888 the Hamilton branch of the Irish National League was dissolved by the executive, which claimed that the branch had acted against its directives in a local election the previous November, when the branch supported Tory candidates. Members of the dissolved branch denied any wrongdoing and claimed that the election was not fought on political lines. This argument, however, was rejected by a number of Irish nationalists in Hamilton, who set up a new, official branch of the League. Members of the dissolved branch did not join this, but continued to argue their case and became known as the 'suppressed branch'. Its dispute with the executive and the official branch continued into 1890.[123] It is not clear when the members of both branches were reunited, but they certainly appear to have been by July 1895, when the *Glasgow Observer* reported the activities of the Hamilton branch of the Irish National League in mobilising the Irish vote behind the Liberals in General Election.[124]

After 1895 the Irish National League in Hamilton went into decline. Reports of its meetings in the press became less frequent. Indeed, in March 1899 the *Glasgow Observer* asked:

> What has become of the INL in Hamilton? No meetings have been held for some time. This does not look very well for the Irishmen of the Ducal Burgh, knowing as they do that they are unrepresented in Parliament. They should be 'up and doing'.[125]

The INL branch at Burnbank was in the same position. In late 1899 a meeting was held under the auspices of the local branch to hear an address from Owen Kiernan, the organiser of the Irish National League, who was touring Scotland at the time, reviving dormant branches and establishing new ones. The *Glasgow Observer* reported that:

> at the conclusion of his address every man present agreed to resume the fight for Ireland by rejoining the League . . . The Irishmen of the district had stood well by the INL during some of the worst years of

division, but recently the League had lapsed. This meeting served as its 'comeback'.[126]

The Burnbank comeback appears to have been a brief one. In May 1905 its branch of the United Irish League (as the Irish National Movement was now known) held a meeting at which its president 'commented on the backward state of the branch and said it was due mainly to the class of supposed patriotic Irishmen in our midst. He explained that the cause they were fighting for needed their help today as much as it ever did, and they would not be worthy Irishmen were they not up and doing'.[127]

By contrast, the Hamilton branch had revived magnificently. The *Glasgow Observer*, in May 1904, announced that in terms of membership the Hamilton branch of the United Irish League 'occupies first place in Lanarkshire, second in Scotland, and fourth in Great Britain . . .'[128] Large attendances were reported for its meetings around this time.[129] Nationalist activity at Cadzow seems to have been rather constant during these years, with the local branch not experiencing any major problems.[130]

From the mid-1900s the United Irish League's position as the leader of Irish nationalism was challenged by the emergence of the Sinn Fein Movement, which advocated a more radical and extreme policy. By 1910 branches of the movement had been established in Glasgow, Motherwell, Coatbridge, Mossend, and Hamilton.[131] The founding of the Sinn Fein Society in Hamilton in late 1908 elicited an immediate response from local nationalists:

> At Sunday's meeting of UIL, held in the Forester's Hall, Church Street – Mr. J. Blaney presiding, a resolution was moved by the secretary, seconded by Mr. Bonner, and passed unanimously, condemning the principles of the new inaugurated branch of the Sinn Fein Society in Hamilton. The members of the local branch of the UIL are of the opinion that the young Irishmen in the district are liable to be misled by the extreme policy promulgated by the Sinn Feiners, and felt it an incumbent duty to record their condemnation at this early stage of the existence of the local branch of the Sinn Fein Society.[132]

This was not the first time the Hamilton nationalists had experienced Sinn Fein. In October 1907, 'One of the largest gatherings of Irishmen ever seen in Hamilton' took place in the Hippodrome Music Hall. The principal speaker was the Irish Nationalist MP, T.P. O'Connor, and the meeting was arranged by the joint branches of the United Irish League in Lanarkshire. Irish nationalists from all over the county attended. While a series of resolutions were being passed, Daniel Branniffe, a Sinn Feiner from Glasgow, approached the platform to move an amendment. According to the *Glasgow Observer* he 'received a most hostile reception, being for some time unable to make himself heard'. After some order had been restored, Branniffe moved, 'that as thirty-six years of Parliamentary policy in Ireland had failed, it was in the best interests of Ireland to withdraw the Irish members from Westminster'. He then attempted to make a speech. This 'was met with a storm of disapproval and loud calls for his removal . . . '. Eventually John Blaney, a leading figure in the Hamilton branch of the United Irish League, escorted Branniffe off the platform.[133] The branch of Sinn Fein at Hamilton, as with the branches established elsewhere, did not, in the years leading up to the outbreak of the First World War, threaten the position of the United Irish League.[134]

Another organisation at this time which sought to convince the Irish nationalists of Hamilton of its views was the Catholic Socialist Society. This body was founded in 1906 by John Wheatley, a former President of the Shettleston Branch of the United Irish League. He later became a cabinet minister in the first Labour government. The aim of the society was to convince Catholics that the doctrines of Socialism and Catholicism were not incompatible.[135] In March 1908, the society held a meeting in the Victoria Hall in Hamilton, which was reported in the *Glasgow Observer*:

> There was a considerable attendance, but some of the speakers were, to say the least of it, unfortunate in their references, which were deeply resented by the audience. There was a continuous flow of interruptions and interjections, and those present showed their disapproval of the entire proceedings in a very marked manner. Ultimately, the promoters of the gathering felt compelled to call in the police, and one of the audience having urged every Irish Catholic in the hall to leave, nearly all retired. There is a feeling of indignation

locally at the attempt to associate Socialism with the Catholic name, and the gentlemen responsible for last Sunday's proceedings would do well to give Hamilton District a wide berth in their future operations.[136]

The absence of any subsequent reports of Catholic Socialist activity in Hamilton in the years to 1914 suggests that the society had a minimal impact on the political beliefs of the Irish nationalists in the parish.

From the mid-1900s until the outbreak of the First World War the United Irish League in Hamilton continued with its activities. It held meetings, socials, and lectures, and mobilised the Irish nationalist vote during the general elections of 1910. Large attendances were reported for these gatherings.[137] When the Home Rule Bill was introduced into the House of Commons in April 1912, the branch organised a large meeting of the Irish nationalists of the parish, at which they expressed their loyalty to the Irish Parliamentary Party and its leader, John Redmond.[138] By contrast, the branches of the UIL at Cadzow and Burnbank appear to have been rather inactive during these years.[139]

The period after the introduction of the Home Rule Bill of 1912 was one of crisis in Ireland. Ulster unionists and Irish nationalists established volunteer armies which armed and drilled. Ulster appeared to be on the verge of civil war.[140] In the west of Scotland Irish nationalists established branches of the Irish Volunteers.[141] One was established in Hamilton in July 1914:

> A meeting of Hamilton Irishmen was held on Sunday last for the purpose of considering the question of inaugurating a branch of the Irish National Volunteer force. Some discussion took place as to whether drills should be held or whether the branch merely aid in the financing of the force, and it was ultimately decided to leave the matter over meantime. Enrolment took place, and over one hundred men pledged themselves to suport [sic] the movement.

John Blaney, William Roarty, and a Mr McLaughlin were appointed as officials of the branch.[142] Blaney and Roarty were leading figures in the Hamilton branch of the United Irish League.[143] The outbreak of war, however, put the political crisis in Ireland on hold for a while.[144]

Large Irish nationalist demonstrations were held in Hamilton in 1898 and 1912. The first of these was organised by the Hamilton branch of the Irish National Foresters and was held to celebrate the centenary of the Irish Rebellion of 1798. Branches of the Foresters within a ten-mile radius of Hamilton were invited, and they marched in procession with their banners and band through the main streets of the town before assembling in West Land Park to hear various speakers.[145] The meeting of 1912 was the occasion of the annual demonstration of the Ancient Order of Hibernians. Over 30,000 nationalists were reported to have taken part in the procession to one of the fields around the town to hear a number of speakers, including two Irish Nationalist MPs. Resolutions were passed congratulating Redmond and the Irish National Parliamentary Party, and the meeting resolved 'to assist them by every means within our power in their endeavours to place the government of Ireland in the hands of the Irish people'. The members of the AOH also pledged their adherence to the Catholic Church. After the demonstration was over, 'the procession of the different contingents, headed by their bands and banners, through the town formed an imposing spectacle, which was witnessed by thousands of spectators. Forty-five different bodies marched in the procession which was led by the famous O'Neill War Pipe Band, Armagh'.[146]

St Patrick's Day was a major event in the calendar of the Catholic community in Hamilton. Here, as occurred elsewhere in the west of Scotland during the era of the Home Rule movement,[147] this annual celebration became a political as well as a religious event. Attendances at the annual soirée and concert at Hamilton were always huge.[148] The speeches by the priests were not only about St Patrick, Ireland, or parish affairs, but were also concerned with the current political situation. For example, in 1883 James Danaher 'spoke of the longevity of the Irish people despite various attempts throughout history to totally exterminate them, and appealed for the cause of Irish nationalism'.[149] Nine years later his successor at St Mary's, Peter Donnelly, after praising St Patrick, told the thousand or so members of his congregation who were packed into Victoria Hall that:

This was the day also, on which they turned to the present temporal condition of Ireland, and, with all the earnestness and patriotism of a persecuted people, longed for her emancipation. In the near and certain advent of a return to power of a Liberal Government he felt they might base their hopes, and trust on having soon, an Ireland and an Irish people as free, prosperous, and happy as a country or nation could be in this world (cheers).[150]

The soirées would usually conclude with a rousing rendition of the then Irish national Anthem, 'God Save Ireland'.[151]

It is not surprising that these priests expressed such views on St Patrick's Day. Donnelly, although born in Greenock was described by a colleague as being 'of a pious Irish stock'. He also spent nine years of his training for the priesthood at Rockwell College, County Tipperary.[152] Like other second or third generation immigrants in Scotland at the time he no doubt felt himself to be just as Irish as those born in Ireland. Danaher was born in County Limerick and trained for the priesthood at Youghal and Dublin.[153] He was one of a number of priests active in the Home Rule Movement.[154] It was said of him that 'he never failed to identify himself with every matter connected with Irish Nationalist Politics, or which tended to raise and strengthen the social and political power of his fellow countrymen. When the occasion called it forth he spoke in defence of the rights of the Irish people with a power and eloquence which awoke the patriotism of his audiences. . . .'[155]

PART 5

In local politics the behaviour of the Catholic community of Hamilton was just as distinct as it was in national politics, certainly from the late nineteenth century onwards. In local elections it worked to mobilise its vote behind favoured candidates, and indeed a number of prominent members of the Catholic community were elected to serve on the local government bodies.

Elected school boards were established in 1873 under the terms of the Education Act of the previous year. Catholic communities in Scotland took an active part in elections to them in order to safeguard Catholic rights and interests.[156] In Hamilton a number of the Catholic priests served on the School Board: James Danaher was a member for ten years, and Peter Donnelly served on it until his death; Emile de Backer, the first priest of the Cadzow Mission, was elected in the 1880s and his brother Louis, who succeeded him at Our Lady and St Anne's, was returned in 1891.[157] By 1906 William McAvoy, Donnelly's successor at St Mary's, and Duncan Brown, priest in charge of St Cuthbert's, were on the board. In 1911 they were joined by James O'Neill, a Catholic layman who was the choice of the congregation at Cadzow. (There were eleven representatives of the school board at this time.) The three were still members by the summer of 1914.[158]

Members of the Catholic community in Hamilton, including a number of the businessmen and professionals discussed earlier, were also elected to the town council and the parish council. On the former body Patrick Small served in the 1880s, and in the following decade James MacHale and William Meechan became members. In 1905 Robert Slorach was elected to the council. He, Small, and Meechan also became magistrates.[159]

In 1894 the Parochial Boards, which had administered poor relief since 1845, were abolished and replaced by elected parish councils.[160] William Meechan was elected to Hamilton's first parish council, as was James Carragher.[161] By the mid-1900s they had been joined on that body by Joseph Lynas and John Blaney. Fr William McAvoy was also a member.[162] Carragher, Lynas, and Blaney were still on the council at the end of 1910, along with three other representatives of the Catholic community, Henry Corns, P.J. McColl, and Peter McConnachie, the priest in charge of the Cadzow Mission.[163] The following April a vacancy on the council was filled by another Catholic, John Cunningham, raising the number of Catholic parish councillors to seven out of a total membership of twenty. According to the *Glasgow Observer*, there was 'not another district in Scotland where the Catholic community has such a large representation on the Parish Council'.[164] By this time Carragher was Chairman of the Council, a position he held until his death in March 1914.[165]

In April 1907 Lynas, Meechan, Carragher, and Slorach became Justices of the Peace for Lanarkshire, along with another prominent Hamilton Catholic, Edward Small, a retired businessman who was also the brother of Patrick Small. Only three other Catholics were among the Justices appointed at this time, one each from Lanark, Blantyre, and Bellshill.[166]

Most of those members of the Catholic community in Hamilton elected to the town council and the parish council were, not surprisingly, also active in Irish nationalist politics and in the church organisations in the parish. Meechan, McHale, Carragher, Lynas, Blaney, Corns, McColl, and Patrick Small all played leading roles in the Hamilton branch of the Irish National League and its successor, the United Irish League.[167] McHale and Lynas both served terms as president of the St Mary's Branch of the League of the Cross.[168] Lynas was also a president of the St Mary's Conference (branch) of the St Vincent de Paul Society.[169] Furthermore, as lay superintendent of the Sunday schools in the 1880s he was the dominant figure in the Christian Doctrine Society,[170] of which Carragher was the treasurer.[171] A James Bradley was active in local Catholic affairs in the 1890s. He served as president of the Hamilton branch of the Irish National League and held the same office in the St Mary's branch of the League of the Cross.[172]

PART 6

Between 1851 and 1855 numerous meetings were held throughout Scotland, at which the Catholic Church and its doctrines were condemned.[173] Michael Condon recalled that in late 1851, 'There was nothing but lecturing against us here, there and everywhere, & misrepresentation of our dogmas, morals and discipline'.[174] Meetings of this kind also occurred in Hamilton,[175] and in 1854 a branch of the Scottish Reformation Society was established in the town.[176] The aim of this organisation, founded in December 1850, was 'to resist the aggressions of Popery, to watch over the designs of its promoters and abettors, and to diffuse sound and scriptural information on the distinctive tenets

of Protestantism and Popery'.[177] Its Hamilton branch held meetings at which Catholicism was attacked. For example, in January
1855 Dr Keith, one of the ministers of the Hamilton Presbytery,
delivered a lecture in the town entitled 'Popery essentially infidel
and immoral'.[178]

Condon did not suffer such attacks in silence. In June 1852,
after one of the itinerant Protestant preachers had spoken in
Hamilton, Condon gave a series of lectures on the doctrines of
the Catholic Church. In his account of the Hamilton Mission he
states that, 'Many Protestants were present. The result generally
was that Prots w^d. sometimes come to be instructed, or bring their
children for baptism'.[179] After Keith's lecture of January 1855,
members of the congregation of St Mary's urged Condon to
respond to it. He agreed, and on 21 January he delivered a lecture
in the chapel to a large audience, which included around two
hundred Protestants. Condon spoke for three hours, during
which time he refuted Keith's charges against the Catholic
Church. Condon was clearly delighted with his performance: 'I
felt I had a triumph and need not defend our dogma or our morals
again'. Keith's lecture was the second of twelve which were
planned by the Scottish Reformation Society. The third was given
a week after Condon's exposition and was intended as a reply to
it. Condon states that the minister's presentation was so unsatis-
factory that the lecture series was 'cut short at the Third. The very
Protestants w^d. hear no more of them. Some of the latter thanked
me for my vindication'.[180]

Over fifty years later, anti-Catholic meetings again aroused
controversy in Hamilton. In April 1909 John Caplain, a lecturer
from the Protestant Alliance, appeared at Hamilton Cross and
delivered speeches against Catholicism. The response of the
town's Catholics to Caplain was a good deal less restrained than
it had been towards his predecessors in the 1850s. A hostile crowd
gathered round him and he had to be escorted by the police to an
awaiting tram-car. According to the *Glasgow Observer*, 'At this
point the crowd made a rush; and but for police intervention
disturbance would certainly have ensued'.[181] The following
Sunday evening, 18 April, Caplain reappeared in the town along
with several followers. Thirty policemen were on duty to prevent

any disturbances. Unfortunately for them, a crowd of 2,000 people were also present when Caplain arrived. The *Glasgow Observer* reported that the preacher 'was received with a shower of eggs and with refuse of all descriptions'. The police formed a cordon around Caplain and his group, and, after some considerable difficulty, took them to the sanctuary of the police station. It was not until after midnight that they were eventually 'smuggled into a motor car and hurriedly driven off'.[182] Two months later Caplain gave a lecture in one of the town's halls and once again received police protection, this time on his way to the railway station. The *Glasgow Observer*, while understanding why Hamilton's Catholics were so upset at the presence of Caplain in their town,[183] argued that they 'would be well advised to steer clear of such gatherings. They are needlessly running the risk of being provoked into breach of the law, and no good can come of the encounter. So long as ranters confine their operations to hired halls, not public property, they should be left severely alone, and in relation to outside gatherings the authorities are able to take care of themselves and certainly should be allowed to do so'.[184] Around this time a society known as the Hamilton Protestant Defence Association was also active in the town. It held meetings and gave lectures against the doctrines of the Catholic Church.[185]

'No Popery' lectures were not the only demonstrations of Protestant hostility towards the Catholic Church and the Catholic community in Hamilton between 1850 and 1914. Condon notes that during the early 1850s his chapel's windows were broken and its garden disturbed.[186] Such acts of vandalism no doubt also occurred in subsequent years. Condon also recalled that he suffered verbal abuse: 'Tho' seldom personally molested, I had, sometimes to run the gauntlet of "To Hell with the Pope etc.", from the Tinsmith's apprentices and the like'.[187]

Yet compared with a number of other areas in the west of Scotland during the period 1850–1914, Hamilton did not experience any major incidents of violent anti-Catholic activity. Home Rule demonstrations in Motherwell in 1873 and 1883, in Coatbridge in 1883, and in Partick in 1875 were attacked by armed Orange mobs. In these and in a number of other towns and villages in the west of Scotland members of the Catholic population were also the victims of sectarian assaults and riots by Orangemen, the overwhelming majority of whom were Irish Protestants or of Irish Protestant descent.[188] Orangeism was strong in those areas where anti-Catholic disturbances took place.[189] By contrast, there is little evidence of Orange activity in Hamilton during this period, which suggests that the number of Irish Protestants in the parish was relatively small.[190] Indeed, in July 1885 the *Hamilton Advertiser* reported that there had been, 'little display or Orange demonstrations in Hamilton, despite much activity elsewhere nearby, the considerable Irish population being Catholic to a man'.[191]

In those areas where violent Orange outrages occurred, members of the Catholic community engaged in similar attacks on Orangemen, Orange marches, and Protestant Irish immigrants. In Hamilton there is also evidence of sectarian violence being initiated by Catholics of the parish. For example, in July 1906 the Blantyre Conservative Flute Band visited the town and entered a public house in Quarry Street:

> On coming out shortly afterwards the band was attacked by a large and hostile crowd. Fighting became general as the band marched along Brandon Street, escorted by a number of the Burgh police, who were kept busy on route separating the combatants. One man, using a catapult was arrested. Fighting continued at intervals all the way to Blantyre where another three men were arrested.[192]

The band had also visited Hamilton the previous month, and disturbances had occurred as a result in Cadzow Street.[193] The band was attacked on both occasions because it was believed that it 'was really the Blantyre Orange band, composed of members associated with Orange Lodges'.[194] As a result of these incidents the burgh authorities issued a proclamation which prohibited any bands from playing in the burgh without their permission.[195]

On at least one occasion, however, Catholics of Hamilton made a mistake in their zeal to ensure that the parish would not suffer from the Orange menace. In December 1879 a Cambuslang band was marching along Brandon Street on its way home from a miners' meeting in Low Quarry. A group of Hamilton Catholics mistook it for a Cambuslang Orange Band known as the 'True

Blue' and attacked the marchers. According to the *Hamilton Advertiser*, 'The Riot lasted from Brandon Street to Peacock Cross, by which time the large drum, and two small ones belonging to the bandsmen were broken and rendered useless'. Four of the ringleaders of the assault, all miners, were convicted for malicious mischief.[196]

Not only is there little evidence of Orange violence against the Catholic community of Hamilton, there also do not seem to have been any major disturbances between Catholics and native Protestants in the parish. The introduction of Irish workers – the majority of whom were Catholics – into the Lanarkshire coalfields in the 1830s and 1840s led to violent conflicts between them and the Scottish miners. This was because the Irish were employed as strike-breakers or as low wage labour.[197] This does not appear to have been the situation in Hamilton. Here, most Irish and Scottish miners entered the pits during the period of the expansion of the mining industry in the parish, which began in the early 1850s:[198] in 1854 there were only eight collieries in Hamilton; by 1878 the number had risen to forty.[199] Strikes did occur at the pits during these years but blacklegs were only used on six occasions during disputes in the mining industry in the west of Scotland between 1856 and 1874, and on five of these occasions they were dismissed by their employers once the strikes were over.[200]

Furthermore, there is evidence that Catholic miners in Hamilton participated in industrial action along with the Scottish miners to protect and improve their pay and conditions. Michael Condon recalls that members of his congregation were involved in the miners' general strike of 1856:

> For several months in 1856, the colliers and miners of my Mission had refused to work, unless their employers increased their wage. Sooner than give in, they preferred, many of them, to live on a meal or two of porridge daily. You might meet their famished faces, here, there and everywhere, collecting subscriptions or asking for a morsel of bread.[201]

In September 1987, the *Glasgow Observer* noted that the congregation of the Cadzow Mission were 'entirely of the mining class', and were therefore not wealthy. It went on to reveal that,

'The seemingly never-ending disputes between master and man did not improve matters, and on more than one occasion the pastor of the mission felt acutely the lack of money'.[202] During the miners' general strike of 1912, the parish of Hamilton was brought to a standstill.[203] The *Glasgow Observer* reported that the great majority of the congregation of St Cuthbert's were 'directly concerned in the coal crisis – many of them being miners on strike . . . '[204] As a consequence of the financial hardship suffered by the miners and their families, the planned celebrations for the Jubilee of St Cuthbert's parish priest, Duncan Brown, were postponed.[205] Similarly, the St Patrick's Day celebrations at St Mary's were also postponed.[206] Free meals were given to the Catholic children by their schools during the duration of the strike.[207]

Indeed, it is probable that those who indulged in the anti-Catholic activities in Hamilton described at the beginning of this section were not representative of the Protestant population of the parish, certainly from the 1870s onwards. At the funeral service for James Danaher on 16 November 1886, 'Several Protestant clergymen, the Provost and the Sheriff, most of the magistrates and Town Councillors, and many of the leading people of the town and district', were among the congregation.[208] The *Glasgow Observer* reported that:

> The town bells were tolled by order of the Provost and the Magistrates, and the flag above the Town Hall was half-mast high. The goodwill and esteem in which the Canon was held by every section of the population were abundantly testified by the large number of ladies and gentlemen, of high social position, who thronged the Church during the celebration of the services for the dead, and the thousands who filled the streets and lined the route to Dalbeth for many miles. Reference to the sad event was made from the pulpits of two Established Churches and one United Presbyterian Church, in a manner which showed in a marked way the good feeling which exists, thanks to him that is gone, between Catholics and Protestants in Hamilton.[209]

Leading members of Hamilton's Protestant population also attended the funeral service for Peter Donnelly in 1902.[210] Seven years later the *Glasgow Observer* reported that when it had become clear that John Caplain intended to return to Hamilton on 18 April to 'preach', William McAvoy 'appreciating the kindly feeling existing amongst all sections of the community, desirous that nothing should be allowed to upset such good relations, and anxious for the preservation of the public peace' had a meeting with the superintendent of police. Its outcome was the decision to have thirty policemen on duty when Caplain returned to the town. The *Glasgow Observer* remarked that in Hamilton, 'the residents live in peace and harmony, and would continue to do so if left to themselves'.[211] In July 1913 Bailie Cassels, who was chairman of the school board, stated at McAvoy's silver jubilee presentation that, 'There had always been in his time the most cordial relations between the Town Council and the School Board on the one hand and the Catholic community on the other'.[212] The following year, when George V visited the town, McAvoy and Robert Slorach were among the guests on the reception platform for the King, and afterwards participated in the celebrations at Hamilton Palace. The *Glasgow Observer* reported that Joseph Seiger, one of the assistant priests at St Mary's, 'and several other prominent Catholic gentlemen were present at the banquet given by Provost Moffat'.[213]

Why such good community relations existed in Hamilton from the 1870s onwards, particularly when compared with the situation in the 1850s, and indeed when compared to other areas in the west of Scotland throughout this period, is not clear.[214] That Irish Catholic immigrants do not appear to have entered the mining industry as strike-breakers, and the evidence of their involvement in industrial action along with Scottish workers, ensured that economic friction did not arise between the two groups. The relative absence of 'Orange and Green' sectarian disturbances in the parish perhaps made the Irish in Hamilton seem less objectionable than elsewhere.[215] In order to explain fully the experience of the Catholic community in Hamilton, however, we need to know much more about the social, economic, political, and religious history of the parish for the period *c.*1850–1914. More work is also needed on Irish immigration to Hamilton; for example, on marriage and residential patterns, trade unionism, and social mobility. Furthermore, in order to place the Catholic community in Hamilton in its context, detailed studies of Catholic communities in other areas in the west of Scotland are needed. Only then will the Catholic experience in Hamilton be fully understood.

References

1. I would like to thank James McKenna for his assistance in the collection of some of the material on which this chapter is based and Mrs Margaret Hastie for typing the manuscript for this chapter.
2. *The Statistical Account of Scotland*, 1791–1799, Vol. VII, Lanarkshire and Renfrewshire (Wakefield, 1973), pp. 397–98.
3. *The New Statistical Account of Scotland*, Vol. VI, Lanark (Edinburgh, 1835), p. 290.
4. *Ibid.* p. 276.
5. For Irish immigration into Scotland see James Handley's, *The Irish in Scotland, 1798–1845* (Cork, 1945), and *The Irish in Modern Scotland* (Cork, 1947). See also Tom Gallagher, *Glasgow, the Uneasy Peace: Religious Tension in Modern Scotland* (Manchester, 1987); T.M. Devine (ed.), *Irish Immigrants and Scottish Society in the Nineteenth and Twentieth Centuries* (Edinburgh, 1991); Alan B. Campbell, *The Lanarkshire Miners: A Social History of their Trade Unions, 1775–1874* (Edinburgh, 1979), especially chapter 7; W.M. Walker, 'Irish Immigrants in Scotland: their Priests, Politics and Parochial Life', *Historical Journal*, 15 (1972), pp. 649–667; W.M. Walker, *Jutepolis: Dundee and its Textile Workers, 1885–1923* (Edinburgh, 1979); Bernard Aspinwall and John F. McCaffrey, 'A Comparative View of the Irish in Edinburgh in the Nineteenth Century' in Roger Swift and Sheridan Gilley (eds.), *The Irish in the Victorian City* (London, 1985), pp. 130–157; Brenda Collins, 'Irish Emigration to Dundee and Paisley during the first half of the Nineteenth Century' in J.M. Goldstrom and L.A. Clarkson (eds.), *Irish Population, Economy and Society* (Oxford, 1981), pp. 195–212; R.D. Lobban, 'The Irish Community in Greenock in the Nineteenth Century', *Irish Geography*, vi (1971), pp. 270–281.
6. See previous chapter.
7. *New Statistical Account*, Lanark, pp. 277, 282; Gordon M. Wilson, 'The Industrialisation of Hamilton', in William Wallace (ed.), *Hamilton 1475–1975* (Hamilton, 1975), pp. 87–89.
8. Norman Murray, *The Scottish Handloom Weaver, 1790–1850: A Social History* (Edinburgh, 1978), pp. 32–33.
9. *New Statistical Account*, Lanark, p. 277.
10. Handley, *Irish in Scotland*, Ch. 4.
11. Glasgow Archdiocesan Archives [GAA], Michael Condon, *Condon Diaries, Hamilton 1850–1859* [hereafter cited as Condon Diaries (Hamilton)], p. 68.
12. *Census of Scotland* 1911, Vol. VI parts 24–37, p. 1379.
13. Condon Diaries (Hamilton), p. 459. 'M. Yarnock' is possibly Meikle Earnock.

14. *Glasgow Free Press*, 20 November 1852, quoted in Handley, *Irish in Modern Scotland*, p. 149.

15. *New Statistical Account*, Lanark, pp. 257–58; Campbell, *Lanarkshire Miners*, p. 149.

16. Robert Duncan, *Steelopolis: The Making of Motherwell c.1750–1939* (Motherwell, 1991), p. 32.

17. Condon Diaries (Hamilton), p. 162; Wilson 'The Industrialisation of Hamilton', pp. 89–92; *The Third Statistical Account of Scotland: The County of Lanark* (Glasgow, 1960), p. 366.

18. Duncan, *Steelopolis*, pp. 21, 26; Condon Diaries (Hamilton), p. 162; *Scottish Catholic Directory*, 1855, p. 89.

19. *Ibid.*, p. 32.

20. *New Statistical Account*, Lanark, p. 269; *Census of Scotland 1871*, Vol. I, p. 74.

21. Duncan, *Steelopolis*, p. 32; *Third Statistical Account*, Lanark, p. 355.

22. Campbell, *Lanarkshire Miners*, p. 295, Wilson, 'The Industrialisation of Hamilton', p. 92.

23. *Glasgow Observer*, 11 November 1905; Kenneth Lunn, 'Reactions to Lithuanian and Polish Immigrants in the Lanarkshire Coalfield, 1880–1914', in Kenneth Lunn (ed.), *Hosts, Immigrants and Minorities: Historical Responses to Newcomers in British Society, 1870–1914* (Folkstone, 1980), pp. 308–342.

24. *Ibid.*, 4 September 1897; 9, 16 March 1912.

25. *Third Statistical Account*, Lanark, p. 366.

26. G.A.A., Annual Returns, MW19, Hamilton Mission, 1869.

27. *Scottish Catholic Directory*, 1860, pp. 87, 88; 1864, p. 103; 1869, p. 99.

28. G.A.A., Annual Returns, MW 19, Hamilton Mission, 1873, 1877.

29. *Scottish Catholic Directory*, 1864, p. 103; *Census of Scotland 1871*, Vol. I, p. 74.

30. *Ibid.*, 1874, p. 95; 1878, p. 93.

31. G.A.A., Annual Returns, MW19, Hamilton Mission, 1877–1883.

32. *Ibid.*, 1877.

33. *Scottish Catholic Directory*, 1873, p. 105; 1879, p. 99.

34. G.A.A., Annual Returns, MW19, Hamilton Mission, 1882.

35. *Scottish Catholic Directory*, 1884, p. 102; 1885, p. 208; *Hamilton Advertiser*, 9 June, 13 September 1883; *Glasgow Observer*, 4 September 1897.

36. *Glasgow Observer*, 4 September 1897.

37. G.A.A., Annual Returns, MW8, Cadzow Mission, 1884.

38. G.A.A., Annual Returns, MW19, Hamilton Mission, 1883.

39. *Ibid.*, 1892.

40. G.A.A., Annual Returns, MW8, Cadzow Mission, 1892.

41. *Scottish Catholic Directory* 1893, p. 188; 1894, p. 234; *Glasgow Observer*, 23 September 1893.

42. G.A.A., Annual Returns, MW7, Burnbank Mission, 1893.

43. See, for example, *Glasgow Observer*, 9, 16, 30 March 1912.

44. G.A.A., Annual Returns, MW19, Hamilton Mission, 1892; MW8, Cadzow Mission, 1892.

45. *Census of Scotland 1891*, Vol. I, pp. 73, 75; *Census of Scotland 1901*, Vol. I, pp. 55–6; *Census of Scotland 1911*, Vol. I, Parts 24–37, p. 1379.

46. Bernard Aspinwall, 'Children of the Dead End: the Formation of the Modern Archdiocese of Glasgow, 1815–1914', *Innes Review*, XLIII, 1992, pp. 128–135.

47. *Glasgow Observer*, 20 April 1907.

48. *Ibid.*

49. *Ibid.*, 4 July 1914.

50. *Ibid.*, 20 April 1907.

51. Bill Murray, *The Old Firm: Sectarianism, Sport and Society in Scotland* (Edinburgh 1984), pp. 25, 68, 71; Brian Wilson, *Celtic: A Century with Honour* (London, 1988), pp. 19, 20, 22, 27, 29, 32, 33, 175, 177.

52. Wilson, *op. cit.*, p. 175.

53. Aspinwall, *op. cit.*, pp. 129–135.

54. G.A.A., *Annual Returns*, MW19, Hamilton Mission, 1878, 1880, 1882.

55. G.A.A., Annual Returns, MW8, Cadzow Mission, 1885.

56. *Glasgow Observer*, 20 April 1907.

57. G.A.A., *Annual Returns*, MW 19, Hamilton Mission, 1885, 1906, 1911; MW 8, Cadzow Mission, 1885; MW 9, Burnbank Mission 1894.

58. Fred Reid, *Keir Hardie*: the Making of a Socialist (London, 1978), p. 47; R Page Arnot, *A History of the Scottish Miners* (London, 1955), p. 115.

59. Parliamentary Papers, 1841 (342), VI, Reports of the Inspectors of Factories to Her Majesty's Principal Secretary of State for the Home Department, for the half-year ending 30 June 1841, pp. 9–10.

60. Condon Diaries (Hamilton), p. 69.

61. See, for example, *Hamilton Advertiser*, 27 September 1879, 2 October 1880.

62. *Scottish Catholic Directory*, 1890, p. 149.

63. *Ibid.*, 1888, p. 166; 1894, p. 171.

64. See, for example, *Hamilton Advertiser*, 27 September 1879, 2 October 1880; *Glasgow Observer*, 4 April, 31 October 1891; 23 January, 6 February 1892; 17 February 1900; 25 November 1911; 27 January 1912; 4 January, 15 February 1913; 17 January 1914.

65. *Glasgow Observer*, 18 October 1890.

66. *Ibid.*, 31 October 1891.

67. *Ibid.*, 18 October 1890.

68. *Ibid.*, 15 February 1913.

69. *Ibid.*, 31 October 1891.

70. *Ibid.*, 4 April, 31 October 1891.

71. *Ibid.*, 31 October 1891.

72. *Ibid.*, 16 January 1892.

73. *Ibid.*, 2 April 1892.

74. *Ibid.*, 16 January 1892.

75. *Ibid.*, 26 March 1892.

76. *Ibid.*, 31 December 1892; *Scottish Catholic Directory*, 1892, p. 177; 1893, p. 188.

77. *Ibid.*, 21 January 1911.

78. *Ibid.*, 27 January 1912.

79. *Ibid.*, 25 November 1911; 27 January, 21 December 1912.

80. *Hamilton Advertiser*, 27 September 1879, 2 October 1880; *Glasgow*

Observer 27 February 1892; 8 April 1911; 4, 11 January 1913; 17 January 1914.

81. *Glasgow Observer*, 23 July 1892.

82. See, for example, *Ibid.*, 21 January, 1 July 1911; 4 January 1913.

83. It is first mentioned in the list of societies for St Mary's in the *Scottish Catholic Directory*, 1881, p. 91.

84. *Glasgow Observer*, 9 May 1885.

85. *Ibid.*, 30 October 1886.

86. It is included on the list of societies at St Mary's in the *Scottish Catholic Directory* until the edition for 1888 (p. 188) and does not reappear on the list until the edition for 1907 (p. 150). The SVDP is not on the list of societies of the Cadzow Mission in the Directories up to 1915, and is only included on the list for the Burnbank Mission in the Directory from the edition for 1904 onwards.

87. *Glasgow Observer*, 15 January 1910; 7, 14 January 1911; 10 May 1913; 24 January 1914.

88. See, for example, *Ibid.*, 1 May 1886, 8 June 1895, 3 February 1900, 14 July 1906; 6, 27 February 1909; 15 January 1910; 25 November 1911; 6 January 1912, 18 January 1913; 10 January 1914.

89. *Ibid.*, 11 May 1895.

90. Lunn, 'Reactions to Lithuanian and Polish Immigrants'.

91. *Ibid.*, pp. 310–13, 317–25.

92. *Ibid.*, p. 309.

93. *Glasgow Observer*, 11 November 1905.

94. *Ibid.*

95. *Ibid.*, 13 January 1906.

96. *Ibid.*, 10 February 1906.

97. *Ibid.*, 21 April 1906.

98. *Scottish Catholic Directory*, 1908, p. 151.

99. *Glasgow Observer*, 6 January 1912.

100. *Ibid.*, 16 March 1912.

101. Lunn, 'Reactions to Lithuanian and Polish Immigrants', pp. 327–29.

102. For Irish immigrants in Scotland and politics, 1850–1914 see Handley, *Irish in Modern Scotland*, Ch. 9; Ian Wood, 'Irish Immigrants and Scottish Radicalism, 1880–1906' in Ian MacDougall (ed.), *Essays in Scottish Labour History* (Edinburgh, 1979); John F. McCaffrey, 'Politics and the Catholic Community since 1878', in David McRoberts (ed.), *Modern Scottish Catholicism 1878–1978* (Glasgow, 1979); Gallagher, *op. cit.*, pp. 62–81; David Howell, *British Workers and the Independent Labour Party, 1888–1906* (Manchester, 1983), Chapter on Scotland.

103. *Hamilton Advertiser*, 24 October 1874.

104. *Glasgow Observer*, 27 October 1894; 28 January, 4 November 1899.

105. Henry Pelling, *Social Geography of British Elections, 1885–1910* (London, 1967), p. 399; *Third Statistical Account*, p. 87.

106. *Third Statistical Account*, p. 87; *Glasgow Observer*, 16 May 1885.

107. *Glasgow Observer*, 6 February 1886.

108. *Ibid.*, 17 July 1886.

109. *Ibid.*, 29 January 1910.

110. *Ibid.*, 3, 12 December 1910.

111. *Ibid.*, 2 January 1886.

112. *Ibid.*, 9, 16, 23 January 1886.

113. McCaffrey, 'Politics and the Catholic Community', p. 150; Howell, *British Workers*, pp. 144–47; Reid, *Keir Hardie*, pp. 108–116; *Glasgow Observer*, 28 April 1888.

114. *Glasgow Observer*, 28 April 1888, quoted in Handley, *Irish in Modern Scotland*, p. 278.

115. Howell, *British Workers*, pp. 154–56; I G C Hutchison, *A Political History of Scotland, 1832–1924: Parties, Elections and Issues* (Edinburgh, 1986), pp. 181–82, 184, 157–58.

116. Duncan, *Steelopolis*, p. 147–48.

117. *Ibid.*, p. 148; Howell, *British Workers*, pp. 164–65.

118. Howell, *British Workers*, pp. 165–66; Wood, Irish Immigrants and Scottish Radicalism, p. 82.

119. *Glasgow Observer*, 28 January, 11 February, 3 March, 8 July, 4 November 1899; 14 April 1900; 2 November 1901; 12 April 1902; 14 February 1903; 13 May 1905; 14 May 1905; 14 May, 10 September 1910; 9 September 1911; 2 May 1914.

120. *Ibid.*, 22, 27 May, 12 June 1886; 25 June 1887; 17 September 1910; 27 September 1913.

121. *Hamilton Advertiser*, 24 October 1874, 29 August 1881; *Glasgow Observer*, 15 August 1896; 14 August 1897; 5 May 1900; 3 May 1902; 5 March 1904; 4 February, 14 October 1905; 21 October 1907; 29 February 1908; 6 April 1910; 27 May, 9 September 1911; 14 September 1912.

122. *Glasgow Observer*, 5 May 1900; 2 November 1901; 6 September 1902; 4 April 1904; 26 October 1907; 4 May 1912.

123. *Ibid.*, 4, 18 February, 15, 22 September 1888; 20 April, 28 September, 12 October, 21, 28 December 1889; 4 January 1890.

124. *Ibid.*, 6, 13, 27 July 1895.

125. *Ibid.*, 4 March 1899.

126. *Ibid.*, 4 November 1899; Handley, *Irish in Modern Scotland*, p. 28.

127. *Ibid.*, 13 May 1905.

128. *Ibid.*, 21 May 1904.

129. *Ibid.*, 6 September 1902; 5 March 1904; 14 October 1905.

130. *Ibid.*, 28 January, 11 February, 11 March, 8 July 1899; 14 April, 5 May 1900; 13 July 1901; 9 April 1904.

131. Handley, *Irish in Modern Scotland*, pp. 291–92; Gallagher, *Glasgow: The Uneasy Peace*, p. 70; Duncan, *Steelopolis*, p. 14; *Glasgow Observer*, 5 December 1908; 16, 23 April 1910.

132. *Glasgow Observer*, 5 December 1908.

133. *Ibid.*, 26 October 1907.

134. See for example, *Glasgow Observer*, 4 May, 7 September 1912.

135. See Ian Wood, *John Wheatley* (Manchester, 1990), especially Ch. 2; Sheridan Gilley, 'Catholics and Socialists in Scotland, 1900–30', in Roger Swift and Sheridan Gilley (eds.), *The Irish in Britain, 1815–1939* (London, 1989).

136. *Glasgow Observer*, 28 March 1908. See also *Ibid.*, 11 April, 1908.

137. *Ibid.*, 21 December 1907; 29 February 1909; 29 January, 5 February, 9 April, 10, 17 September; 3, 17 December 1910; 27 May, 9 September 1911; 4 May, 14 September 1912; 27 September 1913.

138. *Ibid.*, 4 May 1912.

139. There are few reports of their activities in the *Glasgow Observer* of this period.

140. D. George Boyce, *Nineteenth Century Ireland: The Search for Stability* (Dublin, 1990), pp. 233–240.

141. Handley, *Irish in Modern Scotland*, p. 297.

142. *Glasgow Observer*, 18 July 1914.

143. *Ibid.*, 21 May 1904; 10 September 1910; 4 May 1912; 17 May 1913.

144. Boyce, *Nineteenth Century Ireland*, pp. 242–49.

145. *Glasgow Observer*, 11 June 1898.

146. *Ibid.*, 7 September 1912.

147. Handley, *op. cit.*, p. 271; Gallagher, *Glasgow: The Uneasy Peace*, p. 63.

148. For example, see *Hamilton Advertiser*, 17 March 1877, 19 March 1881; *Glasgow Observer*, 26 March 1892, 26 March 1910.

149. *Hamilton Advertiser*, 24 March 1883.

150. *Glasgow Observer*, 26 March 1892.

151. See, for example, *Hamilton Advertiser*, 18 July 1876, 19 March 1881; *Glasgow Observer*, 24 March 1906.

152. *Scottish Catholic Directory*, 1903, pp. 255–56.

153. Bernard J. Canning, *Irish-Born Secular Priests in Scotland, 1829–1879* (Inverness, 1979), pp. 71–74; *Scottish Catholic Directory*, 1888, pp. 189–192.

154. Gallagher, *Glasgow: The Uneasy Peace*, p. 64.

155. Canning, *Irish-Born Secular Priests*, p. 73; See also *Hamilton Advertiser*, 3 April 1875.

156. Handley, *Irish in Modern Scotland*, pp. 218–228; McCaffrey, 'Politics and the Catholic Community', since 1878, pp. 145–46.

157. *Scottish Catholic Directory*, 1888, p. 191; *Glasgow Observer*, 18 April 1885, 25 April 1891, 29 November 1902.

158. *Glasgow Observer*, 17 March, 14 April, 4 May 1906; 1, 8, 15 April 1911; 25 April, 2 May 1914.

159. *Ibid.*, 13 November 1886; 7 September 1889; 23 December 1893; 20 April, 10 August 1907; 17 January 1914.

160. Callum Brown, *The Social History of Religion in Scotland since 1730*, (London, 1987), p. 197.

161. *Glasgow Observer*, 4 April 1895; 20 April, 10 August 1907.

162. *Ibid.*, 10 March 1906; 20 April, 21 December 1907, 5 November 1910.

163. *Ibid.*, 12, 26 November, 31 December 1910, 7 January 1911.

164. *Ibid.*, 8 April 1911.

165. *Ibid.*, 31 December 1910, 16 December 1911, 28 March 1914.

166. *Ibid.*, 20 April 1907.

167. *Ibid.*, 22 May, 30 October 1886; 3 May, 6 September 1902; 20 April, 10 August 1907; 10 September 1910; 9 September 1911.

168. *Ibid.*, 18 October 1890, 12 May 1906, 20 April 1907.

169. *Ibid.*, 20 April 1907.

170. *Ibid.*, 9 May, 12 June 1885; 14 August, 30 October 1886.

171. *Ibid.*, 13 June 1885.

172. *Ibid.*, 30 October 1886, 1 October 1892, 14 August 1897, 6 September 1902.
173. Handley, *Irish in Modern Scotland*, pp. 93–113.
174. Condon Diaries (Hamilton), p. 96.
175. *Ibid.*, pp. 96, 101, 137, 244, 253, 310, 325, 327, 336.
176. *Ibid.*, p. 253.
177. Handley, *Irish in Modern Scotland*, p. 94.
178. Condon Diaries (Hamilton), p. 325.
179. *Ibid.*, p. 137.
180. *Ibid.*, pp. 325–27.
181. *Glasgow Observer*, 17 April 1909.
182. *Ibid.*, 24 April 1909.
183. *Ibid.*, 17 April 1909.
184. *Ibid.*, 19 June 1909.
185. *Ibid.*, 17, 31 July 1909.
186. Condon Diaries (Hamilton), pp. 85, 132.
187. *Ibid.*, p. 262.
188. Campbell, *Lanarkshire Miners*, pp. 178–201, 316–19; Handley, *Irish in Modern Scotland*, pp. 113–17; Duncan, *Steelopolis*, pp. 150–55.
189. Elaine McFarland, *Protestants First: Orangeism in Nineteenth Century Scotland* (Edinburgh, 1990), Chs. 5 and 6. Dundee and Edinburgh, two cities in which the Orange Order was very weak, did not experience any major incidents of sectarian violence during this period. Walker, *Juteopolis*, pp. 120–21; Aspinwall and McCaffrey, 'A Comparative view of the Irish in Edinburgh in the Nineteenth Century', pp. 134, 145; McFarland, *Protestants First*, pp. 73–74.
190. Hamilton is not mentioned in Campbell's list of 'Orange and Green' disturbances in the Lanarkshire coalfield between 1831 and 1883. It is also not mentioned in McFarland's history of Orangeism in Scotland. An examination of the *Hamilton Advertiser* for the month of July from 1867, when the ban on Orange marches in Lanarkshire was lifted, until 1914, reveals only one reference to the presence of Orangeism in the town. This was in 1890 when it was reported that Blantyre and Burnbank Orangemen marched to Hamilton on 12 July to meet up with the Hamilton Orangemen in their lodge room in Quarry Street. They then departed for Wishaw. Campbell, *Lanarkshire Miners*, pp. 316–19; McFarland, *Protestants First, Passim; Hamilton Advertiser*, 19 July 1890.
191. *Hamilton Advertiser*, 18 July 1885.
192. *Ibid.*, 28 July 1906.
193. *Glasgow Observer*, 1906; *Hamilton Advertiser*, 28 July 1906.
194. *Hamilton Advertiser*, 28 July 1906.
195. *Glasgow Observer*, 11 August 1906.
196. *Hamilton Advertiser*, 6 December 1879.
197. Campbell, *Lanarkshire Miners*, pp. 77–84; 181–82.
198. *Ibid.*, p. 295; Wilson, 'The Industrialisation of Hamilton', p. 92.
199. Wilson, 'The Industrialisation of Hamilton', p. 90; *Third Statistical Account*, p. 366.
200. Gordon M. Wilson, 'The Strike Policy of the Miners of the West of Scotland, 1842–74', in Ian MacDougall (ed.), *Essays in Scottish Labour History* (Edinburgh, 1979), p. 56.

201. Condon Diaries (Hamilton), p. 392.
202. *Glasgow Observer*, 4 September 1897.
203. *Ibid.*, 9, 16, 30 March 1912.
204. *Ibid.*, 9 March 1912. See also *Ibid.*, 13 April 1912.
205. *Ibid.*, 30 March 1912.
206. *Ibid.*, 16 March 1912.
207. *Ibid.*, 23, 30 March; 13, 20 April, 1912.
208. *Scottish Catholic Directory*, 1888, p. 191.
209. *Ibid.*, p. 192.
210. *Glasgow Observer*, 29 November 1902.
211. *Ibid.*, 24 April 1909.
212. *Ibid.*, 5 July 1913.
213. *Ibid.*, 18 July 1914.
214. Gallagher, *Glasgow: The Uneasy Peace*, Ch. 1.
215. McFarland, *Protestants First*, p. 107.

CHAPTER 3

Catholic Schooling in Hamilton Before 1918

Mary McHugh

In 1872, the Rev. James Danaher, parish priest of St Mary's, applied to the District Fund for aid to build and furnish a new school. However, the finance board of the Archdiocese regretted its inability to make a grant for the object asked, on account of the large number of other pressing cases. The same reply had been given in 1871, although in 1870 the sum of £20 had been voted from the District Fund to Hamilton, and remained in hand for the new school.[1] In 1874 however, Fr Danaher built a new day school to accommodate 200 children, and in 1882 the school was further extended.

Fr Danaher's schools however, as seen earlier, were not the first Catholic schools in Hamilton. Influential laymen, like Robert Monteith of Carstairs, who made frequent contributions to the Hamilton Mission, believed that education was essential for Catholic survival. Soon after the church opened in 1846, a Sunday school and a circulating library were established. A day and night school existed in 1852, and in 1853 the Hamilton Mission had been able to start a school, partly due to a grant of £20 from the District Fund, some of which was used to furnish the school, while two-thirds was retained to pay the teacher's salary, which was also supplemented by fees of 2d or 1d paid weekly by each of the pupils. Hamilton RC school also received assistance from the Duchess of Hamilton until she retired to Baden-Baden after the death of her husband, and there is no reference to her donation after 1865.[2]

The principle of ecclesiastical control over education was not new, nor was it confined to the Catholic community. In the centuries following the Reformation of 1560, the Church of

Scotland had attempted to establish a network of parochial schools, and by the closing years of the eighteenth century few parishes in the Lowlands were without a school. But the system of parish schools broke down under the pressures of an urbanising society. In addition, many people, particularly the poor, had to be persuaded, and ultimately obliged, to accept that education could be of benefit to them, rather than working from the age of seven upwards to supplement the family income.

Education, both social and academic, was provided by the church, partly through a continuing fear of Protestant proselytism. In 1864, for example, St John's Industrial School, Hamilton, determined that no Catholic pupils would be admitted unless they were willing to learn the Bible and Catechism. Although the policy was reversed one month later, Catholic attendance at non-Catholic schools was actively discouraged by the clergy. In 1884, the headmaster of Low Waters school wrote that 'at least ten pupils (whose parents are Catholics) have been withdrawn from this school and sent to St Mary's, Hamilton';[3] The Rev. James Danaher instructed the parents to remove their children without delay. But such attempts were, it appears, only in part successful. The practice of Catholic children in outlying districts of the parish attending non-Catholic schools continued after the opening of St Mary's school, and even in 1924 the parish announcements included an injunction to parents to send their children to Catholic schools.[4]

By 1870, the Western District as a whole, and the Education Board established by Archbishop Eyre, were viewing with concern the Education Act passed for England and Wales. One major concern aroused by the 1870 Act was the fear, expressed by Cardinal Manning of Westminster, that the new School Boards 'may destroy our lesser schools by reporting them to be insufficient or inefficient'.[5] More trained teachers were therefore urgently required.

In 1870, in Hamilton, the schoolroom occupied the ground floor of the presbytery. However, it was intended that this arrangement should be temporary, as a new school was about to be built. The average attendance was sixty children per week, paying on average 1d each week. The teacher's salary was £34 per annum, comprising £19 from school pence, and £15 from the school manager, Fr Danaher. However, the 22-year-old teacher had been trained at Chalmers and Dick's Western Institute in Glasgow. Until 1894, Scotland had no Catholic teacher training college, and to obtain a Catholic training meant travelling to Liverpool or London. In 1870, there were an estimated 1,800 Catholics in Hamilton, 280 of these aged between 5 and 13, the requisite age-range for attending school under the 1872 Education (Scotland) Act. Nevertheless, the school had only 121 pupils on its roll, and of these only 60 regularly attended.[6]

The new school in Muir Street, Hamilton, opened on 7 January 1873, staffed by one teacher and one pupil-teacher. Though the building had accommodation for 304 pupils, the average attendance was about 200. Fr Danaher visited the school daily and sought to promote attendance, but initially with little effect. The mobility, for example, of railway workers and their families appeared to be one factor discouraging attendance. But the level of attendance was not a unique problem to Catholics either in Hamilton or elsewhere. When Hamilton Burgh School Board surveyed its territory in 1873, actual attendance was found to be 2,080 (1,848 under 13 and 232 over 13) – of which 341 were St Mary's RC. By the early 1880s, the mixed (boys' and girls') school was staffed by a headmistress and two assistant teachers, all of whom were certificated, and by two pupil-teachers. The infants' department had an infant mistress and one assistant teacher, both certificated.[7]

For those scholars who did attend, the inspectors' reports proved increasingly favourable. While in 1873 Her Majesty's Inspectors of Schools, Dr Middleton, Muir, and Calder, had commented on the low numbers presented, and only a weak pass-rate in arithmetic, a year later Mr Andrew considered the work of the children who did attend good and the tone and discipline excellent. By 1880, the standard work was reported to be considerably above the average.[8] One important duty of Her Majesty's Inspectors was to ensure that the government grant was spent wisely and effectively, and they reported therefore on the suitability of school buildings, disposition of desks, books, and apparatus; arrangement of classes, forms of discipline, methods of instruction, attainments of staff, and the quality of moral training. A system of government grants for education had been established in 1833 in England and in 1834 in Scotland, and had been placed under the Committee of the Privy Council on Education in 1839. From 1840, these grants were conditional on government inspection, which was denominational in character, partly due to the need to secure the agreement of the Church of England, and partly a product of the continued educational contribution made by the various denominations. Thus Catholic schools in receipt of grant would be examined by a Catholic inspector. Catholic schools were admitted to the grant system in 1848; and in 1856 the Western District of Scotland joined the Catholic Poor Schools Committee formed in 1847 by the English bishops to negotiate with the government for a share in the annual grants. The purposes for which such grants could be applied had gradually been extended over time. They could be used to maintain the pupil-teacher system and to purchase school equipment or, alternatively, devoted to building more schools, encouraging teacher-training, or maintaining staff housing.[9] But not until 1870 did Fr Danaher, encouraged by the Archbishop, as were other priests throughout the Western District, apply to the Committee of Council on Education, in Downing Street, London, for assistance.[10]

Nevertheless, and notwithstanding the grant position, the continued lack of a training college in Scotland represented a major handicap to the development of Catholic, especially secondary, education, and this became increasingly evident as moves gathered pace throughout the nineteenth century to improve the qualifications and status of the teaching profession. The long-term intention was to abolish the pupil-teacher system which had been introduced in 1846, and which survived until the introduction of the Junior Student scheme sixty years later in 1906. The Junior Student was even more than the half-time pupil-teacher, first and foremost a pupil,[11] with the assumption now being made that their general education would be complete on entry to teacher-training college so that the college course could be devoted to professional studies. Pupil-teachers by contrast had served a five-year 'on-the-job' apprenticeship during which their general education continued. Nevertheless pupil-teachers were expected to provide the main source of supply for the normal school or training college, but few Catholic students, as in Hamilton, proceeded to the three English colleges at Hammersmith, Liverpool, and St Leonards.

Nevertheless, by 1880, efforts to promote attendance were meeting with greater success, to the extent that with an average attendance of 350, the school was now 46 places above its available capacity. In 1882 an extension of two-thirds was opened, which made St Mary's, next only to St John's, the largest school in the burgh. It now had accommodation for 504 children. When Cadzow RC school opened in 1884, it had 250 on its school roll, and relieved some of the pressure on St Mary's.[12]

The period 1884–1918 demonstrated on a larger scale the difficulties which had emerged between 1872–83 – truancy, accommodation, and finance. Even though pithead fees were received from about a dozen collieries, for example £1.16s.10d from Ferniegair, the salaries in 1888 amounted to £394 (£160 for the headteacher; £212 for four assistant teachers; £20 for an articled pupil-teacher; and £4 for a monitor. When materials were added the school outgoings for that year amounted to £690.6s.1d. In 1896, Fr Donnelly approached the Franciscan sisters at Charlotte street in Glasgow, to take over the girls' school at St Mary's, Hamilton, and Sr Philippa arrived in 1896 at a salary of £70 per annum.[13]

By 1908 accommodation problems were again pressing, with, for example, two teachers in one room with 125 pupils. In 1910, an addition to accommodate a further 300 pupils was provided at a cost of £3,000, and one can readily imagine the poor Dean McAvoy's anxiety as he contemplated this considerable, but necessary, financial burden. Some assistance was, however, provided by the Burgh School Board which, in 1909, provided free books, and in 1910 free rubbers, to Catholic, as well as to Board schools. In 1913, against the wishes of the auditor, the Board provided prizes to Catholic schools.[14]

The maintenance of their grant-earning 'efficient' status, therefore, confronted Catholic schools with a series of sometimes contradictory problems. Increased attendances could mean a higher level of grant, but, by the same token, that grant was also dependent upon the existence of satisfactory accommodation, the provision of which inevitably entailed additional expenditure.

The cost of the school added to the debt of the parish. Nor were there bequests or voluntary subscriptions to help pay for the school. The extension in 1882, for example, cost £600, which the parish had to meet. Petitions were sent to both the House of Commons and the House of Lords by Mr James Carragher on behalf of Fr Danaher. The petition to the Commons represented that on grounds of conscience Catholics were unable to attend the public schools, and had to maintain their own schools. And yet these schools had to meet the provisions of educational codes and departmental standards without the benefit of rate aid. But although Mr Ramsay, MP, agreed to present the petition he made it clear that he personally did not support it, asserting that it would advantage one specific group and that he did not wish to see the law changed. Mr Carragher responded that the petition could be applied to all voluntary schools, and was not requesting a change in the law but simply a more equitable distribution of existing funding.[15]

The Catholic case for rate aid found clear expression in a report, dated 27 February 1896, by the sub-committee on voluntary schemes of the Diocesan Education Board. That document claimed that since Catholics were bearing a proportional share with the school boards in the task of national education they were entitled to claim a proportionate share of public support. The claim was reiterated two months later in a memorandum submitted by the Diocesan Education Board to the Scottish Education Department. As Danaher had done, the memorandum restated the Catholic position that the maintenance of their schools was a matter of conscience, and criticised the label 'voluntary' which was attached to them. In Canon Cameron's view, the Church had, on grounds of conscience, no option but to remain outwith the national system. Therefore, Catholic children and parents should not be placed at a disadvantage when compared with the provision made for the rest of the country. Rate aid would enable Catholic schools to improve the accommodation and education presently provided, while, at the same time, removing a double burden of payment from the Catholic community.[16]

Having admitted the need for rate aid, and having conceded the corresponding principle of transfer, a permanent solution to the financial problems confronting the Catholic voluntary schools became a possibility. However, the eventual 1918 Education (Scotland) Act was preceded by many false dawns. Efforts to arrive at a national solution were pre-empted by a local initiative from the Glasgow School Board in 1910. Under its proposal, which did offer to the Catholic schools the benefits of rate aid, voluntary schools were to be leased to the Board for a period of ninety-nine years. However, it was quickly realised that as one board could not bind its successors, legislative sanction was necessary to ensure continuity of policy.[17]

Discussions and counter-proposals continued throughout the years of the First World War. Catholic deputations were repeatedly cautioned not to hope for any increase in grants, and this difficulty over grants brought into sharper focus the need for an agreement on terms of transfer for the voluntary schools, a need which became more urgent when further educational reforms were proposed. Internal pressures were also posing difficulties for the Catholic voluntary system. Catholic teachers were consistently paid less than their counterparts in board schools. Indeed by 1908–09, salaries were lower even than their 1880 levels. By 1908–09, the salaries of the teachers at St Mary's stood at £102 for the headteacher and twenty assistant teachers at salaries ranging from £40 to £88.[18] In addition, as the West of Scotland Catholic Teachers' Association made clear, in the matter of superannuation and pension provision for their eventual retirement, Catholic teachers desired that they should receive 'equitable treatment' in comparison with their colleagues in board schools.[19] Moreover, by 1917, the teachers felt excluded from the Church's decision-making processes, claiming that they 'were not taken into the confidence of their priest managers'. As Sister Mary of St Wilfrid, Principal of Notre Dame Training College, bluntly informed Mgr Brown the Apostolic Visitor, in December 1917, 'things are as bad as they can be; the managers have broken faith . . . Archbishop Maguire has withdrawn his patronage from the

Catholic Teachers' Association, the authorities (Archbishop and Vicar-General) refuse to receive a deputation from the teachers, so do the Rev Managers. It is a perfect impasse'.[20] Just how grave the situation had become can be demonstrated by the fact that some teachers had considered the possibility of a general strike, and of releasing correspondence on the dispute to the public press.

Catholic concerns about the 1918 Act focused on four main areas: the control of religious instruction, representation on school management committees, the appointment and dismissal of teachers, and the provision of new schools. Compromise on most points was, however, necessary, but the emerging solution was threatened by the response of the Archdiocese of Glasgow. According to a deputation of teachers to the Scottish Education Department in February 1918

> The Archbishop has given instructions that in his diocese anybody who likes to speak against the Bill is to have a free hand . . . The Catholic newspaper in the West, the *Glasgow Observer*, is controlled by the Archbishop, and is doing all it can to discredit the proposals of the Bill. As a result, Catholic opinion is being thoroughly misinformed as to the Government's intentions, the insinuations being that the professions and offers put forward are wholly insincere.[21]

The Apostolic Visitor, Mgr Brown, also urged the Catholic community to accept the Bill, for ' . . . if we incur the odium of wrecking this Bill we handicap ourselves in every effort to induce another Government to pass one even as good for us'.[22] Even so, at this late stage the passage of the bill was threatened when the Cathedral Chapter and senior priests of the Archdiocese of Glasgow renewed their demands, including that school managers, rather than the new education authorities, should retain control over the appointment and dismissal of teachers. Only the intervention of the Holy See, which insisted that the majority decision of Bishops, clergy, and laity to accept the bill be upheld, averted the danger, and allowed Mgr Brown to signify to the Scottish Secretary the Catholic community's acceptance of the bill, which received the royal assent on 21 November 1918. It became the basis of modern Catholic education in Hamilton as elsewhere in Scotland.

References

1. Glasgow Archdiocesan Archives (hereafter GAA), FRI/1 Minute Book of the Finance Board, 1869–91.

2. Catherine Collins, 'The Development of Education in Hamilton with particular reference to the period of the School Boards, 1872–1918', Ed.B (Hons) thesis, June 1965, p. 129.

3. *Ibid.*

4. Announcement Books, St Mary's, Hamilton 1918–25.

5. A.C.F. Beales, 'The Struggle for the Schools', in Bishop George Andrew Beck, *The English Catholics: A Century of Progress (ed.) (London, 1950)*, p. 376.

6. Collins, 'Development of Education', p. 130.

7. *Ibid.*, p. 133

8. *Ibid.*, p. 130.

9. GAA, ED5, 'How the Presbyterian Schools were Financed'.

10. GAA, ED9, Western District Board of Education, printed regulations for grants, having accepted the Rules of the Catholic Education Crisis Fund Committee, undated.

11. James Scotland, *The History of Scottish Education*, Vol. 2 (London, 1969), p. 113.

12. Collins, 'Development of Education', p. 133.

13. *Ibid.*, p. 136.

14. *Ibid.*, p. 140.

15. *Ibid.*, pp. 133–34.

16. GAA, ED2, Diocesan Education Board, Report by Sub-Committee on Voluntary Schemes, 27 February 1896.

17. James Handley, *Irish in Modern Scotland* (Cork University Press, 1947), p. 237.

18. Collins, 'Development of Education', p. 140.

19. GAA, ED28 Charles McKay to Archbishop Maguire, 8 December 1907.

20. GAA, ED16 Sister Mary of St Wilfrid (Mary Adela Lescher) to Monsignor Brown, 3 December 1917.

21. Brother Kenneth, 'The Education (Scotland) Act 1918 in the Making', *Innes Review* Vol. XIX, No. 2 (1968), p. 112.

22. *Ibid.*, p. 123.

CHAPTER 4
St Mary's Church

James Douglas

The first reference to the restoration of a Roman Catholic congregation is in a Catholic Directory of 1831 where it states that 'one of the Glasgow clergy officiates once a month in Hamilton, a small town ten miles distant, where from three to four hundred persons attend divine service'. This Hamilton 'mission' embraced the middle and upper (i.e. southern) wards of the county. As seen in Chapter 1, in 1843 the Rev. John Scanlan was appointed the first resident priest, and in 1845 the Rev. James Purcell began the erection of a church which was opened by the Rt. Rev. Bishop Murdoch on the first Sunday of Advent, 29 November 1846. The two clergy stationed in Hamilton had to extend their work to places as far afield as Carluke, Lanark and Carnwath, and other localities.

The Church Building Fund accounts indicate the areas from which collections came in, e.g., Blantyre, Kilbride, Uddingston, Bellshill, Motherwell and district, Strathaven, Larkhall, and Shotts. With the advent of the iron and steel works about twenty parishes sprang up, which were at some time dependent on St Mary's Hamilton.

The Church was solidly built of sandstone, and is typical of the period, i.e., pseudo-Gothic with a rather good façade, originally with more pinnacles than at present. It was a pleasing enough building inside, with long, polished windows and a spacious nave unobstructed by pillars. The stone altar, consecrated in 1857, was a present from the Duchess of Hamilton (Princess Marie of Baden). Princess Marie made several other gifts to the Church, including a chalice, monstrance, candlesticks, and vases. There was also fitted up for her own use 'a magnificent and costly pew, furnished with elegant chairs and *prie-dieu* . . . and a beautiful plaster statue of the Virgin and Child adorns the recess of the sanctuary.' This statue of 'Our Lady of Victories' was later placed above the altar. A notable feature of the chancel was a fine picture portraying the 'Adoration of the Shepherds', which came from the Hamilton Collection. It is a 16th-century copy of a painting by Tibaldi; the original is claimed by the Borghese Gallery in Rome. An elaborate canopy hung above the altar. Such was the general picture of the church up to the end of the nineteenth century.

By 1890 it became necessary, because of the growth of the congregation, to enlarge the accommodation, which was originally intended for 600 people. The incumbent, the Rev. Peter Donnelly, took the bold, but perhaps doubtful step, of erecting a gallery. This provided 200 extra seats, but it rather spoiled the pleasant features of the interior by the erection of supporting pillars. At the same time a new wooden roof was erected to replace the original plaster one; this is the same roof to-day and it is considered to be a very fine one.

The Very Rev. Dean McAvoy, the successor, had shortened four of the windows on the right (south) side of the church to allow for the erection of three confessionals. At the same time a new clergy-house was built with a school and hall (the original presbytery was part of the church building on the South side). At the east end of the church, on either side of the reredos, are two pleasing stained-glass windows. On the right hand is one of Our Lady and St Charles Borromeo; underneath are the letters AMDG with the title 'in memory of Charles George Archibald, 2nd son of William, 11th Duke of Hamilton, died 3rd May, 1886, aged 39'. The left-hand window portrays the Apostle James as a figure with a pilgrim's staff and a gourd, carrying a book in his right hand. Beside him is 'Christ the Good Shepherd'. The inscription reads: 'In memory of Canon James Danaher, 27 years pastor of this church who died 15th November, 1886. R.I.P.' The makers were Mayer & Co., Munich and London.

The centenary of the Church was celebrated in 1946, but because of the War there were no elaborate changes or celebrations. However, in 1949 building restrictions began to ease and in that year the late Monsignor Hamilton was responsible for several additions to the north-facing wall. A stone porch, a place for the baptismal font, and a chapel for the repose of the remains of the dead were provided, and a new hardwood floor was laid.

Several changes in the chancel were also completed around this time. The old stone altar had to be removed, along with the painting, and a replacement of alabaster and marble was installed against the east wall. A magnificent replica of the Crucifixion was erected, and the walls of the sanctuary were panelled in English oak. Two side altars were erected and statues of the Sacred Heart and Our Lady filled the walls on either side. The fronts of the galleries were redecorated and adorned with the 'arms' of Pius XI and XII, four Archbishops of Glasgow, and Bishop Murdoch and Bishop Douglas of the new diocese of Motherwell.

In 1975 the interior was redecorated. The altar was brought forward in the chancel to accord with the new presentation of the liturgy. An attractive floor was laid in the aisles and new benches replaced the ones which served for over a generation. In 1990–91 the main windows were found to be in such poor condition that it was decided they should be renewed.

As the Church is called St Mary's it seemed only right that we should honour Our Lady in one of the windows. The stained-glass window at the front (Epistle side) depicts the Immaculate Conception and the Assumption. To balance the windows, a stained-glass window depicting the Sacred Heart was installed in the opposite side (Gospel side).

CHAPTER 5

Intermarriage, Education, and Discrimination

Joseph M. Bradley

The next two chapters will consider a number of social and political issues relating to the people of St Mary's' parish today. Most evidence reflects the emerging Catholic community in west central Scotland, primarily Irish, with a few from the north of Scotland, as being an impoverished one. Despite some individual successes, mainly focusing on those who initiated personal services as entrepreneurs and shopkeepers, the Irish Catholic immigrant community of the 19th and early 20th centuries was socially and economically amongst the very lowest orders.[1]

Politically speaking, although they gradually supported the Labour Party as it emerged in the new century, their preoccupation was also with the historical relationship between their country of origin and Britain. Ireland had been steadily colonised by the English/British over a period of hundreds of years, but particularly since the plantations of the early 17th century, when many of those given Irish land by the British Crown were Protestants from Scotland. Rebellion against the British has been an inherent part of Irish history, and a perception of Irish disengagement from British rule (a rule that was often viewed as being the prime cause of their hardships and the reason why they departed Ireland) remained with the Irish wherever they went. In particular, since the days of Daniel O'Connell, many Irish communities in Britain either engaged in political agitation for some form of Irish independence, or they took part in the more militant activities that sometimes coincided.

It is unlikely that St Mary's parishioners were any different from their counterparts across the Irish Catholic communities of Lanarkshire and the greater Glasgow area, the region where the vast majority of the immigrants settled, and indeed where most of their offspring in Scotland remain today. Nonetheless, increasing secularisation, the length of time the Irish have been in Scotland, marriage outside of the community and pressure to conform to the ways of the host community have all had an effect upon the identity of the present Catholic community in Scotland. It does not remain the cohesive populace it was once considered. However, as I have shown elsewhere, it does survive as a distinctive ethnic community, with its own political and cultural identity.[2]

In 1990 I conducted a survey of a number of groups in Scottish society, but particularly, football supporters, Catholic Church attenders and Church of Scotland attenders. Although it was only partially representative, many of its conclusions correlated with similar works. This survey looked at the attitudes and activities of these groups in relation to questions concerning Northern Ireland, British political parties, Scotland's constitutional future, football teams, the monarchy, etc,. Religious, occupational, and social profiles were also constructed. Although all Protestants do not share attitudes, the survey concluded that there were clear differences between those of a Protestant and those of a Catholic background. Parts of the subsequent text will broaden the scope of the St Mary's material by using some of this survey for comparison.

Over the course of the latter half of 1994 I undertook to administer a questionnaire to a sample of the current parishioners of St Mary's. Many of the questions contained in the 1990 survey were repeated in the St Mary's context. Table 1 shows that around fifty per cent of parishioners were regular mass attenders in 1994, which is in fact above the Scottish average of approximately 35 per cent (the parish is made up of 1800 people). One hundred and twenty-eight mass attenders were subject to the questionnaire (between 10 July and 14 August) along with other parish members who volunteered to complete the survey away from the church or who were interviewed on pre-arranged visits (an estimated 7 per cent of St Mary's' mass attenders came from outwith the parish). In addition, I complemented the data with a series of interviews; around three dozen adults (aged 17 to 92 years) and about two dozen young people of Holy Cross High

School in Hamilton (who were also part of the parish). Finally, some questionnaires as well as a few interviews were conducted among non-church-attending members of the parish. The data deal with residence, education, employment, politics, cultural affinities, and opinions on two crucial issues for Catholics today – abortion and the maintenance of distinctive Catholic schools.

Table 1. Numbers Attending Mass (at 16 October 1994)

6.30 p.m. (vigil)	175
10.00 a.m.	260
11.30 a.m.	285
6.30 p.m.	180
Total	900

Table 2. Age of Church Attenders and Percentages Attending

Age (years)	Per cent
Under 24	17
25–34	20
35–44	20
45–54	14
55–64	12
65+	16

Some General Features

Of the 128 mass attenders surveyed there was almost an even spread between women and men. Sixty of the respondents were male and 65 were women. In terms of the age profile of the attending parishioners there was a similar representation (Table 2).

These results are similar to the findings of the 1990 study of twenty-two Catholic parishes.

With the assistance of the current parish priest, the author divided the parish into nine areas. However, some areas (around one quarter) in which the respondents lived were unclear from the data. Nonetheless, some idea did emerge of where mass attenders in the parish originated. Many came from two districts of the parish. Sixteen per cent of mass attenders came from the central area of Hamilton; that is, the district around Duke Street, Low Patrick Street, and Leechlee Road. Sixteen per cent also came from the newer estates which surround Carlisle Road, known locally as Barncluith. Twelve per cent of attenders originated from the area around Silvertonhill (including, Laburnum, Abercorn,

Portland, Cheviot, Larch, etc). Almost one in ten (nine per cent) came from areas in or near Chantinghall, Burnbank Road, the Allanshaw Industrial Estate and nearby Bent Cemetery. Smaller percentages of people came from the Auchingramont Road area, the locality surrounding Almada Street, Kemp Street, Bent Road and Tuphal Road areas, as well as the Douglas Park and Hamilton College neighbourhoods. However, the smallest percentage (2 per cent) of mass attenders surveyed resided in an area previously viewed as part of the backbone of the parish. The area known as the 'Old Town' (Old Toun) is only a few hundred yards from the church; it contains a few hundred Catholic families within it, but fails to provide a corresponding number of attenders. During the course of interviews it was impressed upon the writer that it is a deprived and impoverished locality.

Almost three-quarters (69 per cent) of mass-attending parishioners surveyed were born in Lanarkshire; forty per cent of them in Hamilton. Another one in five (19 per cent) were born in Glasgow. Five per cent were born in other parts of Scotland, whilst seven per cent were born outside of Scotland; India, England (2), Wales, Italy, USA, and Poland being the countries represented. In terms of a comparison with the first decades of the parish, when in common with most other parishes it was built by Irish labour and finance, the most dramatic fall in representation has been the figure for those 'born' in Ireland. Only two per cent of current parishioners of St Mary's were born there.

'Intermarriage'

Around half of 'Catholic' marriages in Scotland takes place with a partner who is not of the Catholic faith.[3] In Northern Ireland the figure is around 9 per cent which, to a degree, reflects the more intense political and cultural nature of such a union there. Others might argue, that it also reflects a greater depth of faith on the part of many Catholics in Ireland (the figure for England is about 70 per cent).[4]

However, one interesting fact to emerge from the St Mary's survey is that the vast majority of Church attenders – 87 per cent

1. St Mary's Church in its original 19th-century form.

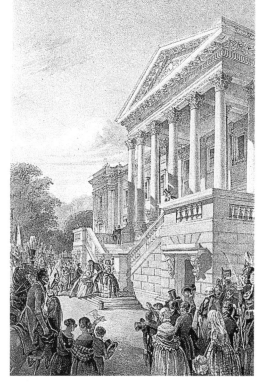

2. Reception of the Marquis of Douglas and Princess Marie of Baden, Hamilton Palace, September 1843. Princess Marie became an important benefactor of St Mary's Church.

5. Low Waters, 1897.

3. Hamilton Old Town Residents, 1890.

4. Meikle Earnock Pump Well, 1890.

6. Cadzow Street, 1893.

8. Sheiling Hill, 1890.

7. Old Cross, looking down Castle Street on Fair Day, 1880.

9. New Cross, 1893.

10. Hamilton Town Hall, 1897.

11. *Adoration of the Shepherds*: This 16th-century copy of a painting by Tibaldi adorns the chancel of St Mary's Church. It came from the collections of the Duke of Hamilton. In the 1850s the Duchess of Hamilton (Princess Marie of Baden) was a generous benefactor of St Mary's and regularly attended mass there.

12. Main altar: This shows the gallery erected by the Rev. Peter Donnelly in 1890 to accommodate another 200 people, a reflection of the rising parish numbers of the time. The two stained-glass windows are those referred to on page 81.

13. Dean McAvoy, Parish Priest; Miss M. Murphy and class of St Mary's School, 1927.

14. Funeral of Dean McAvoy. The cortège forms up outside St Mary's Church.

15. St Mary's Pipe Band at the funeral of Dean McAvoy in Bothwell Road.

16. St Mary's Pipe Band.

17. St Mary's Boys' Guild, *c.* 1925–30.

18. St Mary's first communicants with Monsignor Hamilton, Parish Priest, 1963.

come from families where both parents are Catholic. Four per-
cent had a Catholic father and a non-Catholic mother; five per
cent had a Catholic mother and non-Catholic father, and two per
cent had both parents as non Catholics; therefore almost all
respondents had Catholic parents.

One of the conclusions from the 1990 data was that it app
eared that the vast majority of Catholic church attenders had two
Catholic parents. This is confirmed by the St Mary's statistics. In
relation to the figures for mixed marriages, the overall suggestion
is that among Catholics who are falling away from the church, a
large number will come from those who marry outside of the
faith; i.e., they are very likely either to continue not attending
church or to stop going.

This hypothesis is further reinforced when one considers the
answers to the religious denomination of respondents' married
partners. Almost one-third of respondents were unmarried
(Table 3).

*Table 3. Religious Denomination of
Partner*

Denomination	Percent
Church of Scotland	4
Other Protestant	3
Roman Catholic	62
No religion	3

When unmarried people are excluded from the survey it is found
that 86 per cent of Catholics married a Catholic partner. The
figure correlates with the 85 per cent of partners who were
brought up as Catholic. The latter figure gives a picture that
spreads throughout the various generations.Therefore, it suggests that the chances of a Catholic remaining practising are
greatly increased when that person marries someone who is also
a Catholic. It would seem to be the case that a process of

reinforcing a partner's religion occurs for many Catholics embarking on marriage. It certainly provides a barrier against a lapse in faith. In relation to these figures (and those from the 1990 survey) the conclusion must be that 'mixed marriages' are a contributing factor towards Catholics becoming irregular or non-church-attending, and indeed is an element in the process of the secularisation of today's Catholic community in Scotland.

Class and Education

Undoubtedly, the Catholic Irish occupied the lowest strata of Scottish society for many decades. However, as education and employment opportunities have changed for the working classes and the wider society, particularly in the post Second World War period, Catholics have shared in much of the progress (despite the clear indications of general poverty and a growing 'underclass' in the late 20th century).

Certainly, if we consider the 'Catholic church attenders' of St Mary's today, they appear to be a very well educated group. The vast majority of them have achieved Scottish certificates of education; one in four achieved one or two highers and one quarter merited three or four (only one respondent from the Old Town church attenders and non-church-attenders – apart from two school attenders – had attained any highers). Similarly, almost half had attended university or college and acquired a degree-level qualification, or were presently studying for one. In the wider survey conducted in 1990 only sixteen per cent of Catholic Church respondents had attained a degree compared to almost one in four of Church of Scotland respondents. The St Mary's 'church attenders' stand out as comparatively well educated.

In terms of employment status the vast majority were profes-sional or technical workers (44 per cent), while 12 per cent were involved in management or administration. Only 16 per cent of respondents were involved in semi-skilled or manual employment (Table 4). These figures are well above those of all the Catholic groups surveyed in 1990, thus emphasising St Mary's parish (in terms of its church attending constituency) as clearly 'middle class' in composition, justified by educational attainment and employment status.

Table 4. Employment of St Mary's Respondents

	Per cent
Skilled manual	7
Semi or unskilled manual	9
Professional or technical	44
Management/administration	12
Clerical	5
Sales	7
Never had a job	1
School/student	11
Unemployed	3

Table 5. Father's Work

	Per cent
Skilled manual	28
Semi or unskilled manual	33
Professional or technical	20
Management/administration	11
Clerical	4
Sales	4

Table 6. Employment of 'Other' Catholic Church Respondents[5]

	Per cent
Skilled manual	19
Semi or unskilled manual	19
Professional or technical	22
Management/administration	9
Clerical	14
Sales	7
Never had a job	1
School/student	8

Table 7. Employment of Church of Scotland Respondents[6]

	Per cent
Skilled manual	14
Semi or unskilled manual	9
Professional or technical	32
Management/administration	8
Clerical	24
Sales	7
Unemployed	6

Table 8. Employment of Supporters of Celtic FC[7]

	Per cent
Skilled manual	31
Semi or unskilled manual	24
Professional or technical	20
Management/administration	8
Clerical	6
Sales	6
School/student	4

Catholics, and the working class generally, have shared in this century's rise in living standards and increased opportunities despite the continued existence of poverty and underclass entrapment.[8] Indeed, the latter have been referred to as particularly affecting Catholic sections of the population in Scotland.[9] Changes in economic and employment conditions have resulted in a growth of white-collar jobs and a decline in manual work and Table 4 clearly shows that Catholics have permeated all strata of employment.

Table 5 reflects the upward movement of Catholics in the parish; on the whole many have moved away from the traditional employment of their fathers, almost three in five of whom were involved in manual work. Catholic groups surveyed show that their community provided the economy with vast numbers of its unskilled manual labour in previous generations. The St Mary's respondents have become educated and moved into the professions. Overall, although Catholics still predominate in the lower ends of the employment market (see Tables 6, 7, 8), clearly the church-attending parishioners of St Mary's are exceptional in the strides they have taken within the past generation.

Prior to this study, anecdotal evidence suggested that St Mary's would not emerge as a typical Catholic parish, at least in the sense that quite a number of its members were in the teaching profession or were self-employed. These impressions are confirmed by the evidence. Nonetheless, despite the professional status of many of its members, and regardless of the corresponding material advantages, such as good housing and car ownership, the author did sense that these church members retained many of the attitudes often viewed as characterising the working class. This will be reflected in Chapter 6 when we look at the political dimensions of the community. Also, it is an echo of the weaker traditional class barriers in a cultural Catholicism, that the vast majority of the Catholic community have shared through the generations, previously one reflecting the perception and experience of a downtrodden and impoverished community.

Discrimination

Related to questions of employment is the historical perception within the Catholic community of a society in Scotland characterised by anti-Catholicism. One of the ways this sectarianism has traditionally manifested itself is in an exclusion from better employment as well as from many institutions, professions, and occupations. That this perception still holds is demonstrated in the figures which emerged from the survey in 1990 (in which St Mary's parishioners also participated). Almost half of Catholic church-attenders in that study believed that Protestants rather than Catholics would be favoured in the workplace; nearly three-quarters of Celtic fans believed so with about the same figures for the Irish bodies also surveyed, and ironically this was concurred by almost one-third of Glasgow Rangers fans and ten per cent of Church of Scotland attenders.

Almost half of today's St Mary's church-attenders believe that discrimination in favour of Protestants is a social reality in

Scotland. Despite the clear upward social mobility of the St Mary's parishioners (which may have meant the breaking down of barriers), and slightly over half not believing that religion is a factor in determining employment, the figure of 45 per cent is a significant one, especially if it is taken alongside the other groups surveyed.

These perceptions were somewhat substantiated on interviewing a cohort of the St Mary's parish. Only two of these respondents did not acknowledge sectarianism in the workplace. All of the others either had experienced it, knew of someone who had experienced it, or had heard about it.

A number of shops, companies, and establishments were mentioned as being bastions of anti-Catholicism or as having discriminatory practices in the past. Although many of these have now gone or have been taken over by English or US companies, some are still in evidence in the area. Several had signs in their windows stating 'No Catholic Need Apply'. The list is both local and national. It included Lanarkshire Steel Works, the police, the Electricity Board, Fisher's General Store, Gibson's Fruiterers, King's sweet factory in Wishaw, The Clydesdale Bank and other banks, Harland and Wolfe and other shipyards, Finleystone's Engineering Works in Bellshill, Babcox and Wilcox in Renfrew, Walker's the Drapers in Hamilton, Colville's Steel Works, Hastie's the Bakers, Glasgow University, the local Council, Tunnocks, Dalziel the Bakers, Anderson Boyce Engineering Works in Motherwell, some elements of the west of Scotland mercantile class, and a number of bowling and golf clubs in the area.

One respondent stated that 'in the past it was atrocious. If there was a job vacant, no Catholic need apply'. Another remembered a group of Catholic men challenging some shops on their policies many years ago. One respondent, a professional in his fifties, said that in his dealings with the banks over the years it took until the 1980s before he dealt with a Roman Catholic. An older parishioner explained that he only got a job (around the time of the Second World War) because a left-wing Protestant friend got him one. A younger interviewee related the experience of his father, who could not join the police in the 1950s because he was a Catholic, while he believed he had been shielded from the worst excesses of discrimination because the family had its own business.

One lady in her seventies could remember people advertising for home help with the addendum that no Catholics need apply. Another parishioner who worked in Glasgow's shipyards spoke of Catholics being confined to the construction of one boat, while he had experience of being a shop steward and fighting to have anti-Catholic symbols removed from the factory surroundings. He concluded; 'For anybody to tell you it doesn't exist they're talking rubbish. Maybe it's not to the same extent, but it's rife'. An older respondent believed that, 'things have not changed. It's the masonic thing, it's still there, though Catholics are not frightened anymore'. A young St Mary's member believed that in the local council many of the better jobs were held by non-Catholics with the Catholics being employed in less meaningful work.

There was a consensus that things were not as bad as they once were, and this was due to the growth of English and multinational companies (Stepek, the Co-op, and Woolworth were mentioned) which were less inclined to discriminatory practices, i.e., they were not under the control of anti-Catholic Protestants. Some respondents also believed that a sound Catholic education and working-class access to higher education had improved the lot of Catholics. Many still believed that discrimination existed but that it was less obvious and often had to be carried out in secret. Overall, there is a clear and widespread perception throughout both the St Mary's and the wider Catholic community that discrimination against them in the workplace was a factor in Scottish life, and still exists to a degree.

References

1. See, B. Aspinwall, 'Children of the Dead End: the Formation of the Modern Archdiocese of Glasgow, 1815–1914,' in *The Innes Review*, Vol. XLIII, No. 2, Autumn, pp. 119–144, 1992. The accounts by such people as Brother James Handley, *The Irish in Scotland* (Cork, 1943 & 1947), or even later of T Gallagher, *Glasgow: The Uneasy Peace* (Manchester 1987), reflects well the situation that the immigrants encountered.

2. See Joseph M. Bradley, *Ethnic and Religious Identity in Modern Scotland*, (Avebury, Aldershot, 1995.)

3. Information from Catholic Archdiocese, Glasgow.

4. See A. P. Purcell, *Our Faith Story* (1985,) p. 123.

5. Survey carried out by the author, 1990.

6. *Ibid.*

7. *Ibid.*

8. See article by Brian Wilson, *Herald*, p. 16, 17th Feb 1995.

9. Puzzle of Prison Catholics' Bill Rankine, *Sunday Observer, Scotland*, 9/4/89. Also, around the same time, the Chief Inspector of prisons in Scotland carried out a random survey, finding 35 per cent of the inmates Catholic. This was linked to urban alienation whilst one priest commented that the 'figures fitted in with greater poverty and deprivation still experienced by Catholics in Scotland'. BBC Radio Scotland, 'Speaking Out' 12/7/90.

CHAPTER 6

St Mary's Parishioners Today: Politics, Schools, Moral Issues, and Ireland

Joseph M. Bradley

In the 19th century there was a strong Irish attachment to the Liberal Party, mainly because of its adherence to Irish Home Rule and Conservative hostility to Ireland and Catholics in general.[1] However, as the 20th century developed, social and economic conditions in Scotland began to be challenged by many of the working classes, including the Irish. As much of Ireland was to gain its independence in 1921–22, and with the civil war in Ireland causing much grief to the Irish abroad, they began to turn towards the Labour Party, a party that was viewed as being moulded in the best interests of the poor and the disadvantaged. Subsequently, many writers have referred to the close relationship between Catholics and Labour in Scotland for much of this century. Indeed, it is reckoned that the Labour Party has been such a strong force in Scotland/Britain primarily because of this bonding.[2]

Although Catholics viewed Labour as a political vehicle to assist them in raising their standard of living and in gaining a degree of equality in Scottish society, this was not reflected in their representation at some levels of the party. The sensitivities of Protestants and secularists within Labour meant that for years its dominant figures recognised that to have Catholic candidates would have been detrimental to the Party. Indeed,

> Catholic MPs were few in Scotland, only three, so far as one can judge, from the electoral guides in 1919–39 and only more numerous from the 1960s onwards. Even at the local government level, while they were more numerous, election results indicate they were fewer than their proportion in the population.[3]

Nonetheless, observers such as Brand have demonstrated that the Catholic attachment to Labour and the commensurate lack of identity with other parties have given Labour a strong electoral base in west central Scotland.[4] My own general survey of Catholic church-attenders in 1990 showed that 66 per cent of them adhered to Labour, a figure which rose even more dramatically to 85 per cent where the figure for Celtic supporters was concerned. Six per cent of respondents supported the Conservatives and 8 per cent the SNP. Such figures demonstrate the affinity of Catholics in Scotland for Labour, though the figure for Catholic church-attenders also shows a decrease in attachment which may reflect the emergence of a Catholic 'floating' or issue voter, and a more salient social and moral agenda involving questions of abortion and Catholic schooling. Church of Scotland figures in 1990 showed that only 22 per cent of them supported Labour, 11 per cent the SNP, and one in three as Conservative supporters (Table 1). Giving some credence to Miller's claim that it is often the irreligious who are SNP adherents,[5] the SNP support in the 1990 survey was also found to originate mainly with non-church-going respondents, thus marking them as a party with a high percentage of secular adherence.

Table 1. *Church of Scotland Political Party Support*[6]

Party	Per cent
Labour	22
Liberal Democrats	11
Conservative	34
SNP	11
Social Democrats	2
None	19

With reference to the St Mary's respondents, almost 60 per cent of them reported themselves Labour supporters, only 8 per cent as Conservative, 12 per cent SNP, and 6 per cent Liberal Democrat. In addition, those parishioners outside of the main body of the survey (i.e., those still at school, older irregular church-going parishioners, and the unchurched of the parish) also indicated 60 per cent support for Labour. None chose the Conservatives or the SNP. The rest adhered to no specific party. Therefore, despite St Mary's parishioners being better educated and having entered better employment, and the increasing prominence of moral questions on the political agenda, they still retained a strong attachment to Labour. The percentage of Labour supporters also rose in terms of the non-church attenders.

Nonetheless, a series of interviews with St Mary's respondents also revealed that few of them were 'passionate' Labour supporters, though they had even less time for the other parties. There was a general feeling of disillusionment with British politics, that many politicians were the same, regardless of party, and that Labour 'were the best of a bad lot'. Most interviewees felt that in the past Labour had been good on 'social justice' themes and had helped Catholics in their own economic and social struggles.

A number of respondents displayed apprehension over abortion policy within Labour, and viewed the party as being a pro-abortion organisation. Likewise, some Labour representatives were viewed negatively for their perceived support for the ending of Catholic schooling; two respondents viewed the Conservatives as being better on these issues. One interviewee claimed, 'Labour have probably done more for Catholics than any other party, primarily because there have been a lot of Catholics involved with it. At the end of the day, politicians are self-seeking. They don't support Catholics the way they should on abortion'. A seventy-three-year old female respondent believed that Labour were 'bad on moral matters. Homosexuality and pornography is being allowed by them. On social things and working-class matters they're good'. An older parishioner believed that 'Labour wouldn't help Catholics now. They are all educated men now and not working men rising up'.

A seventeen-year-old parishioner of St Mary's stated that her mother was a Labour activist, though she herself was not politically aware. For the moment her attachment to Labour was a family one. One fifty-seven-year-old male interviewee remembered some priests trying to encourage their parishioners to support the Conservatives, because of the Communist influence on Labour. However, the Communists that he knew remained practising Catholics.

The wider 1990 results for Catholic respondents demonstrated that few Catholics support the SNP. Indeed, Brand has stressed that the SNP are relatively weak where there is a strong Catholic population in Scotland, i.e., in the west central belt. The SNP are again found to lack support in St Mary's parish, though they have a more significant support here than in other Catholic areas of Scotland.

A hallmark of the SNP since its foundation has been its goal of an independent Scotland. However, almost all of the groups surveyed in 1990 did not agree with that (less than one in five), over one-third believing an Assembly a better option and a little less than a third believing Scotland should be better understood. Seventy per cent of Catholic church-attenders surveyed in 1990 believed Scotland should have an Assembly, while 80 per cent of Church of Scotland attenders thought likewise. The latter figures approximate to the results of various surveys in recent years.[7]

On this question, St Mary's respondents were not unlike other groups surveyed. Sixty-eight per cent believed Scotland should be better understood or have an Assembly while 19 per cent support independence. Nonetheless, the question of Scottish independence has been part of a Catholic psyche in Scotland which has traditionally been characterised by widespread apprehension. St Mary's interviewees were asked their opinions in the event of an independent Scotland.

About a fifth of St Mary's respondents either believed that a Northern Ireland situation would be created where the Protestant population dominated the Catholics and excluded them from many areas of social, economic, and political life. A number of respondents also feared for Catholic schools. A respondent in his twenties offered the view that 'maybe it would cause trouble, maybe like Northern Ireland. Maybe they would look for another enemy if England is gone. There is a lot of prejudice on both sides and it may well fire it up. It's quite scary to think about it'. Another parishioner, a lady in her forties, expressed a general fear, 'schools, Churches upkeep, etc.'. A younger parishioner also relayed a concern over schools: 'I'm not sure how Catholic schools would get on; they would be my major worry'.

An older parishioner had no worries at all, believing that Catholics now had power and they could not be abused. A woman in her eighties also believed that Catholics 'could look after themselves now', whilst another respondent believed that since the establishment was not Protestant anymore, there would be little to fear. Nonetheless, there was a fear or apprehension expressed for the position of Catholics in an independent Scotland, though like the general population, most Catholics, and St Mary's parishioners in particular, would like to see a Scottish Assembly or a Scotland better understood within Britain.

Questions of the Day: Schools

Any contemporary student of Catholic affairs in Scotland will observe that divisive questions regarding the maintenance of Catholic schools and the issue of abortion are crucial questions. Elsewhere, I have considered much of the debate as conveyed by those who support the schools and those who are against them.[8] Most of the Protestant churches in Scotland are implicitly or explicitly against, though a number of individual Protestants (including some ministers) have expressed their worth in the 'fight' against secularism. In addition, there is a growing lobby among secularists (including humanists, atheists, and agnostics) who also wish them to be removed. There are also some Catholics who would like to see them ended.

The Labour and Conservative parties follow a similar line on the issue, both stressing that they prefer all schools to be non-denominational; but, so long as Catholics wish to maintain the schools then the parties will defend them. The SNP are of a similar opinion, though it was in fact a prominent representative of theirs who indicated support for the schools in the strongest terms. In 1992, Jim Sillars stated that:

> The charge of divisiveness against the Catholic community is a tactic employed by those whose true intention is not integration – but the abolition of Catholic schools.

Bigotry he says, continues to exist:

> and pop up in the most unexpected of places, sometime disguised as liberal thinking. . . . The day Scotland is relaxed enough to recognise separate Catholic schools as the absolute right of a community which contributes to the enrichment of our national life and ethics, and is therefore not questioned as to its rights, Scotland will have arrived.

For Sillars, Catholic schools are:

> a test of whether the non-Catholic majority is able to acknowledge the laudable tenacity with which the Catholic community holds to its faith in an increasingly secular society.[9]

Despite such affirmations, some Catholic cynics believe Sillars was simply playing the 'Catholic card', in an attempt to gain Catholic votes throughout west-central Scotland and break the mould of the Catholic attachment to Labour. Indeed, the then Catholic Archbishop of Glasgow welcomed Sillars's remarks but was unsure whether they represented the views of the party at large (Sillars lost his seat and announced his disillusion with politics). Cardinal Winning for example, noted that in 1982, the then president of the SNP, William Wolfe, expressed a number of perceived anti-Catholic statements (Wolfe voiced fears for the Falkland Islanders, mainly Protestant and of Scottish extraction, who he suggested were at the mercy of the Catholic Argentinians. Wolfe also criticised those who allowed the Pope to visit Scotland in 1982).[10] Former SNP parliamentary candidate, Hamish Watt, was also known to be strongly against Catholic schools in the same period.

In the 1990s, Strathclyde Region's Education Committee has been at the centre of these altercations over Catholic schooling, the issue contentiously re-emerging due to falling school rolls, lack of finance, and the perceived need to increase school size to broaden subject choice for pupils. Subsequently, the Education Committee has closed down a number of schools and amalgamated others. However, this has also created a problem where the local Catholic school has been closed and pupils are left with a choice of having to travel a further distance to the nearest Catholic school available or transferring to a non-Catholic school. In other instances, non-Catholic children may find that their nearest school is a Roman Catholic one. This may mean that there are more non-Catholics than Catholics in a 'Catholic school' (schools must accept children of any or no faith). Thus the idea of a Catholic ethos in a 'Catholic school' becomes nonsensical for many Catholics. Some Catholics view such moves as an insidious way of dismantling Catholic schools. The views of some Labour councillors in Glasgow, who generally view the integration of schools as a social and political goal, give some credibility to these fears of the Catholic hierarchy and laypeople.[11]

Catholic defensiveness is increased by the generally held beliefs of the Educational Institute of Scotland (EIS), the schoolteachers' main trade union. A motion passed at conference in 1979 displaying opposition to Catholic schooling, resulted in a large proportion of their Catholic membership threatening to leave the union. In a speech in 1985, the retiring president of the EIS also criticised Catholic schools, stating:

> The segregation of children only five years old on religious grounds is wrong, grossly so. . . In this matter the law is not merely an ass but an assassin. . . The results. . . the tribalism of broken heads at Hampden and the broken hearts of couples whose plans to marry in good faith have been defeated by prejudice, are unacceptable to the majority of the Scottish people.[12]

The then Archbishop (now Cardinal) Winning countered, by stating:

> It shows what the Catholic community have to put up with from people who I believe have no time for religion in schools.[13]

A number of options were put to the St Mary's attendants regarding the schools' question; each respondent was allowed to answer positively to three of the six answers. Eighty-four per cent of respondents believed that in a free society Catholics should be allowed to educate their children in a Catholic way. Forty-six per cent expressed the view that bigotry existed before Catholic schools and they were not to blame for its existence in Scotland. Twenty-seven per cent of parishioners believed that Scotland is quite an anti-Catholic country, and many people here would do anything to weaken the Catholic faith, while 65 per cent of respondents supported the schools because they viewed them as central to Catholics. They were, said one respondent, 'important in a world that cares little for God, so that their children could be reared in the Catholic faith'.

Those more opposed to Catholic schools were represented by 6 per cent who thought they 'caused bigotry and sectarianism and should be abolished'. Five per cent of parishioners believed that 'they were not needed anymore and Catholics should be educated along with children of any and of no religion'.

These results were confirmed over the course of interviews. One 17-year-old, presently attending the local Holy Cross High School, believed that if there were no Catholic schools the faith 'would go to pieces. They would be left to think for themselves. The Catholic faith would be weaker and moral values would be affected'. A seventy-year-old respondent said that if the schools had to end, 'it would be a worse situation than we are in now. I don't think the kids being brought up now are all that interested in religion. The situation is getting worse over religion'.

In fact, many others expressed a similar sentiment; that they were displeased at the state of religion in schools and in society generally, and it would deteriorate further if there was any change in circumstances. Such a view was prevalent among all the age groups interviewed. Another popular sentiment was that 'I think the Catholic population would fall; though I know many kids who go to Catholic schools but have no interaction with the faith'. Also, 'a sparse Catholic education would result in a decline. RE provision is poor even now in schools'. Similar views were suggested by a lady in her forties: 'Catholicism is declining and people are making up their own rules. Society is making the rules and it's the main factor in influencing people much more than schools. If not, then the situation would be worse; some contact [through the schools] is better than none'. One fifty-seven-year-old parishioner concurred: 'The Church of Scotland will disappear if they don't bring religion back into the educational system. The family is vital but schools shape the kids whether we like it or not'.

Most of those of the fifth and sixth year at Holy Cross and who are parishioners of St Mary's also supported Catholic schools. 'It would break down' (i.e., the Catholic faith) if there were no Catholic schools; 'I think there would be trouble, it would be bad for the faith'; 'I feel that although a lot of people don't go to mass, they've still got a strong faith; its nurtured at school, it's as basic as school graces, being nice to people and things; People need an element of the Catholic faith', and 'we would lose the Catholic faith'. Although some 16- and 17-year-olds at school voiced the opinion that RE at school was a waste of time for them, most enjoyed the experience. Indeed, it seemed to be the case that positive or negative feelings on the subject were largely determined by the teacher.

Contrary to much of the opinion expressed in the media, and, at least in relation to the church-going parishioners of St Mary's, the overall conclusion arising from these figures and interviews is that there is overwhelming local support for the retention of Catholic schools where they exist in Scotland. Indeed, the support is striking in its coherence and in its uniformity. In addition, the arguments in support of the schools on the part of many, if not most Catholics, focus on the development and growth of a secular Scottish/British society which is viewed as modern Catholicism's greatest enemy.

Abortion

Abortion can be viewed as one of the main moral questions for the Catholic Church in the latter part of the 20th century. Like the schools, it is also a divisive issue in Scottish and British society, one that has a cultural, social, and political dimension to it.

It is also apparent that the issue threatens the relationship that Catholics have traditionally had with Labour. The main political parties in the country have similar policies on abortion, in that they support the 1967 Act which many Catholics believe has led to abortion on demand. However, Catholics have invested much time and commitment in three-quarters of a century of the Labour Party, and some feel that the Party is using and abusing their support in a way that goes against their beliefs.

Indeed, in 1991 the Labour Party banned the anti-abortion grouping, 'Labour Life', because the pressure group's policy went against party policy. Archbishop Winning responded to Labour on behalf of the Catholic Church in Scotland:

> The pro-life credentials of individual candidates and of political parties should, I believe, play a crucial role in deciding who we vote for . . . We should think long and hard before we vote for someone who is prepared to permit the killing of unborn babies.

The editorial of the official journal of the Archdiocese of Glasgow, *Flourish*, continued the Archbishop's theme, but, in addition, took the political dimension of the argument a step further:

> Is Labour, any more than any other party, best poised to reflect our Christian priorities? The dilemma is evident in its grudging attitude to Catholic schools but it is thrown into sharper relief by its pro-abortion policy – an issue which no Catholic can regard as marginal . . . Significantly, during voting on that Bill [the Embryo Act], several Labour MPs stood at the entrance to the pro-life lobby making the Sign of the Cross, whilst jeering at others, saying 'the Pope says go that way . . . The time has come for Catholics to make their views known to the party which traditionally expects their support: the time has come to let it be known that "care" can never mean "kill".'[14]

The press, as well as at least one Catholic Labour MP in Scotland (who is in fact against abortion), criticised Winning for interfering in politics and attempting to influence party political choice.[15]

As far as Winning is concerned he is attempting to raise a fundamental issue of Catholic moral and social belief to a higher political platform. Winning believes that if housing, nuclear weapons, education, and perceived cutbacks in the NHS are issues of political and moral importance, then even more so is abortion, particularly given that; 'one in five pregnancies in Britain now ends in abortion'.[16] Of course, this belief is shared by many ordinary Catholics and a number of Catholic Labour MPs.[17] The Archbishop argues that he is attempting to educate Catholics to vote, not out of habit, but based on what MPs and parties say about issues. Winning argues that Catholics, like anyone else, have a right to use the opportunity 'to shape the parties we have'.[18]

The Labour Party in Scotland remained relatively silent amid the furore.[19] For some Catholics, this may reflect the party's concern that if such religious-related matters became key political issues they might lose much of their Catholic constituency.[20] One leading British newspaper commented upon the link in Scotland between these issues and religious identity in society. It pointed out that 'mixing abortion, Labour and the Roman Catholic Church makes a powerful west of Scotland cocktail'.[21]

The 'attack' by Winning and *Flourish* was not simply an attack on Labour or an attempt to introduce morality into politics on one issue. Since its founding in the late 1970s, *Flourish* has also emphasised what it regards as the lack of a moral element in the policies of the Conservative Government. Arguments against the Government's perceived cutbacks in the health service,[22] their treatment of the poor[23] and Government sanctions policy on South Africa,[24] have been a recurring theme.

Catholics' letters to the press were generally supportive of the Archbishop; this illustrating a high degree of support for an anti-abortion stance amongst the community itself.[25] Several believed that it was crucial that the issue should have an important place on the political agenda:

> Any political ideology which considers unborn life to be part of the Age of the Disposable must be confronted. Archbishop Thomas Winning, president of the Conference of Bishops of Scotland, has chosen to do so now, not a day too early . . . It is commonplace for politicians to set the political agenda: this stratagem is a usurpation of the role of the electorate.[26]

Future Scottish Shadow Secretary, Tom Clarke, contributed to the debate by writing for the *Catholic Observer*, following the publication of the controversial *Flourish* article. Ironically, Clarke fully supported the Archbishop's stance. He also resurrected a key element in the 'old' Catholic identity by making an appeal to the Catholicism and socialism of John Wheatley, arguing that Catholic hopes and aspirations for 'improving the quality of life' were still to be best found in the Labour Party.[27] Here an issue with direct religious overtones can be seen to possess the capacity to create another dimension to political cleavage in Scotland, as well as to influence a possible re-alignment of voters.

The parishioners of St Mary's were also asked their opinion on the question of abortion. Seventy-two per cent of respondents agreed with the survey question: 'Do you believe in the teachings of the Catholic faith that abortion is always wrong, except when the life of the mother is threatened?' In addition, the same percentage of parishioners believed that 'from the moment of conception everyone is one of God's children'.

Contrary to this stance, 10 per cent of church-attenders at St Mary's agreed that abortion is a 'woman's right to choose'. Only 2 per cent of those surveyed agreed that abortion was an acceptable method to control the world's population.

Although there remains some deviance from the general Catholic arguments against abortion, it is clear that a large majority of church-attenders of St Mary's are united in their opposition to abortion. Again the statistical evidence was given further credibility when a number of parishioners elaborated on their opinions on abortion.

Many respondents believed that television and the media were pro-abortion. A seventy-three-year-old parishioner believed that was the case. She stressed that the media influenced thinking: 'people don't think for themselves and believe all they read in the papers. SPUC films are not allowed on TV which means they are censored'. Some people believed that the media were in fact afraid of the issue. One parishioner in his twenties said, 'the media accepts abortion; it's totally for it. If we didn't have the faith and we were taking our information from the TV then we would all support abortion. Most MPs are pro-abortion'.

Another man in his fifties stated that 'generally speaking, I think the media has helped create the climate where it is accepted and in some cases promoted'. A similarly-aged women respondent perceived the media as 'pushing it, and if you're against it on soaps and such things then they always show you to be a Catholic'.

A member of the St Mary's parish in his sixties argued that, 'the media is supporting it, and the media's influence would lead them to allow euthanasia. I do sympathise with young girls' problems today though'. Another older woman believed that, 'the media, they're for it. Contraception should rule out abortion today. The media had a lot to do with the law changing in 1967'.

Those attending the local school were not unlike their elders in their view of abortion. One girl in fifth year said that, 'The media is trying to show it as an option. Some people are brought up to see it as an option. There are other options and there's too much advertising for abortion as well'. 'The media is mostly for it, pro-choice and women's movements and things like that' said a male pupil. A schoolmate considered, 'I feel they're very biased towards the woman's choice, the freedom of choice. They don't care so much for the child'. 'They seem to suggest it's a woman's choice, they're more pro-abortion', argued a female pupil.

There is a recognition of the problems that arise from a sexually promiscuous society, and some sympathy for the predicaments of young girls who view their lives as being out of their control if they encounter pregnancy. Nonetheless, throughout the various age-groups of the St Mary's respondents, there is a clear and unambiguous opposition towards abortion in today's society.

Ireland

As with other developing Catholic parishes in west central Scotland St Mary's owes its existence to the arrival of Irish immigrants during the 19th century. The spread of the Irish diaspora due to economic, political, and religious factors in Ireland, meant that the core identity of Catholicism also spread to Britain and the USA.

The political, cultural, and social identity of today's Catholics in Scotland has been a matter of some debate in recent years.[28] Important in this debate has been the relationship between second, third, and fourth generation Catholics in Scotland to their country of origin, Ireland. Elsewhere, I cover the debate in much greater detail.[29] Suffice to state briefly some of the characteristics of both the Irish identity of Catholics in Scotland and some of the features of the debate.

One of the key problems with much of the literature is that it operates with a narrow understanding of religious identity by using sectarianism as its key concept. As such, some authors ignore the multi-faceted nature of religious identity in Scotland. Such a culturally and socially dominating orthodoxy has resulted in a confusing, and indeed, an inarticulate Irishness (as well as Scottishness) within the present Catholic community in Scotland.

In fact, some newspapers carry periodic criticism of Catholics who express an Irish identity, especially if it is seen as being at the expense of a Scottish identity. This can be seen to reflect a lack of clarity in Catholic social and cultural identity. It also indicates the complexity of modern Catholic or immigrant Irish culture in Scotland.

After one such perceived attack upon the Irish identity in Scotland (in the *Scottish Catholic Observer*), a number of readers answered back:[30]

> Not for a long time have I witnessed the heritage of possibly 90% of Catholics in Scotland being so overtly dismissed and disregarded, if not indeed attacked . . . Most of my own social experiences here in Scotland are still very much of an Irish kind.[31]

> How close one wants to stay to one's roots is of course a personal decision and the ethnic Irish certainly don't need any lectures on 'valuing Irish ancestry above a Scottish birth'. It is hardly the function of a Catholic paper nor indeed of the Church to tell people where their loyalties should lie. Too many people in the Church in Scotland are ashamed of, and want to hide our Irish ancestry, this is why we never hear them decrying those of Italian or Polish descent who are not all that bothered about a Scottish birth either.[32]

The problem of the 'Irish identity' is in part a continuing legacy of the controversies between the native Scots Catholic clergy in the 19th century and Irish Catholic immigrants. However, in more recent times it is more significantly connected with inter-pretations of the 'Troubles' in Northern Ireland, as well as popular British/Scottish perceptions of things Irish.

Although it is apparent that extensive Catholic involvement in agitation for a perceived free and independent Ireland largely ended with the creation of the Free State in the 1920s, and that since then, activity to promote the 're-unification' of the country has been minimal and limited, the general 1990 survey reflects the undoubted desire of the offspring of the Irish for re-unification.

The links between the Catholic community and Celtic Football Club are well documented.[33] In my survey, almost four in five Catholic male church-attenders stated that they supported Celtic Football Club. Indeed, even among the few women who were football supporters over three in five concurred. Among Irish cultural and political bodies the figures were even higher.

Events involving Celtic supporters have long been characterised by songs and emblems which aspire to an Ireland disengaged from perceived British domination. The 1990 figures suggest that this attitude permeates the wider Catholic community in Scotland, and in a way that other sections of Scottish society are not influenced (most other sections involved in the survey either supported Northern Ireland being part of the British Union, or they were unsure of their opinion). Almost 70 per cent of Catholic church-attenders and almost 80 per cent of Celtic supporters support a united Ireland according to the 1990 data.

In terms of St Mary's respondents, almost 70 per cent of them support a united Ireland, 16 per cent don't know, while only 7 per cent believe in the Unionist ideal. Additional questions put to the interviewees were intended further to analyse Catholic perceptions of the Ireland-Britain problem.

Although the St Mary's parishioners strongly support a united Ireland, they have disparate views on the origins of the problem and of how it is developing. A 73-three year old female stated that, 'it was Britain in the beginning, but I'm totally against the IRA methods and killing doesn't solve anything'. An 80-year old male church-attender said, 'I have sympathy with the aims of the IRA but not their methods. The Unionists are impostors from Scotland. Northern Ireland was always totally undemocratic and the Unionists hid behind the British Government'. One parishioner of Italian descent believed that, 'the British Government is to blame, though I would be scared if they withdrew. I don't know if there will be an end to it'. A parishioner in his fifties who had previously been a member of the Anti-Partition League also blamed Britain.

Some parishioners were quite passionate on the subject. One man in his sixties stressed that, 'the problem is one of British forces occupying Ireland. It may take another civil war to sort it out; so be it. Let the Irish people sort it out themselves'. One lady in her eighties whose parents had come from county Mayo said, 'England took the north of Ireland and many other countries. The whole of Ireland is Irish, though now with the English it's all confused. The north never belonged to Britain'.

Although less articulate than the older generations, pupils at Holy Cross expressed similar views to their elders. One 16-year-old girl argued; 'It's moved away from the original issue of occupation, slaughter, and killing of Irish people. The British had no right to be in Ireland. But now the Troubles are about terrorism and bombs. The past has to be remembered if they're talking about it, but its like extremists in Iraq and Iran now'. A male pupil of the same age said, 'The UK is to blame. They should have let them get on with their own lives, 'cause its a different country anyway'.

One lady in her forties was quite clear on her perceptions: ' A united Ireland would be an ideal situation, but I see that the Protestants have a point of view. Money is a problem. Better for Catholics but not for Protestants. Historically the British are to blame, but it's more complex today'. One teenager had a similar viewpoint, 'All solutions seem to have a downfall though a united Ireland seems the best one'. Another respondent believed that the 'resolution will lie in demography. All of Ireland has to be included in a democratic referendum. Protestants will start to leave and come to Scotland. Not the end of the Troubles, but they will change'.

A striking feature about much of the younger perceptions was the part that television (often concerned and pre-occupied with questions of violence) has to play in their ideas. Indeed, this would also be the case with many of the older generations. Nonetheless, a number of young people were honest in that they stressed how uninformed they were about the whole situation. Overall, it is clear that the ideal of a united Ireland still retains strong support among the offspring of Irish immigrants in Scotland.

One of the conclusions of my previous work was that apart

from such things as intermarriage with Protestants and those of no faith, Europeanisation, secularism, as well as the length of time that many Irish have been in Scotland, a culturally dominating orthodoxy has made it difficult for many Catholics to maintain an Irish identity. Anti-Catholicism and the popular association of many Irish cultural-religious features with sectarianism has meant that Irishness has been a repressed identity,[34] one which has lacked esteem and articulation as a result.[35] This has meant that Celtic Football Club has for many Catholics become a 'safe', and indeed for some, the only condition or situation where an Irish identity is popularly manifest.

The lack of an Irish identity for many Catholics is less surprising when one considers that there has always been little or no reference to Ireland in a school curriculum (or indeed in third-level education) in Britain/Scotland which stresses a common Anglo-Saxon and Scottish heritage. In the past: 'the teaching of subjects other than religion differed very little in Catholic elementary schools'.[36] Thus, if the British and/or Scottish identity was being reinforced via the education system for the indigenous population, it invariably had a negative effect upon the Irish identity. The education system has not only helped integration, but has facilitated assimilation.

Historically, in Scotland the Irish and Catholic identities have been primarily undermined by their unacceptability to society. Irish and Catholic are clearly not the interchangeable terms they once were, though for those of an explicit anti-Catholic disposition, they remain so. Although in some societies identity can be strengthened in the face of antagonism, the conclusions of Hickman and of Curtis suggest that in Britain, large numbers of Irish people have underplayed their Irish, and in some circumstances Catholic, identity. Likewise, while the writer was carrying out the empirical part of the 1990 study some Catholic interviewees expressed their inhibitions in calling their children by Irish/Catholic forenames. In some instances the Irish part of their identity was too difficult for them to recognise; they were inclined more towards a Scottish name or a name that had little to do with a conscious identity. In other cases however, the reason that 'my child would never get a job', or 'I don't want to be bigoted', were forwarded as the rationale for such decisions. Therefore, for many Catholics in Scotland the Irish identity is a submerged one.

Nevertheless, the strength of Irish identity is still significant in the Scottish west central belt. Indeed, a cursory look at the wider context of Celtic Football Club is only one, though the most indicative of ways to form an impression of its strength. Nonetheless, the 1990 survey showed that many people have indeed become confused regarding their identity. Possibly because of negative associations in Scotland/Britain of things Irish, but even in terms of simply identifying their heritage or ethnic background, they often fail to establish a clear picture. This confusion (or the miscomprehension of the question) was displayed a number of times in the 1990 survey when some individuals on reporting their background-heritage as 'Scottish', were further investigated, and asked by the interviewer their names and where their grandparents etc., originated. Lennon, McCann and McHara, three of the respondents (all Irish names, none coming from a mixed religious marriage), were found to have between them, one Irish born parent, at least five known Irish born grandparents, whilst McHara was reminded by a friend that his family had come to Scotland from Armagh. Despite the answers which stated Scottish, ethnically speaking the respondents were in fact Irish.

Although the vast majority of Catholics in Scotland originated from Ireland, only 42 per cent of Catholic Church attenders in 1990 identified themselves as being from an Irish background; 15 per cent said an Irish/Scottish one, and 37 per cent of attenders reported themselves as having a Scottish background. The rest were made up of a mixture of identities or very small numbers of other traditions. Celtic football supporters were more Irish minded but even here the figures are lower than what might be expected. Fifty eight per cent said Irish and 2 per cent Irish and Scottish. Thirty four per cent reported Scottish only.

With reference to the Irishness of those of St Mary's parish, similar results emerged over the course of this study. The St Mary's figures were not unlike the broader findings reported. Almost 40 per cent stated they were from an Irish background while 20 per cent suggested an Irish-Scottish one. Twenty-seven per cent referred to a Scottish heritage. The process of interviewing parishioners revealed more information.

The interviewing process proved a more appropriate setting to explore the question of ethnicity. Most interviewees appeared to be aware of their Irishness; most indeed designated themselves as having an Irish background. Nonetheless, similar problems to those encountered in the 1990 survey arose. For example, one respondent in her sixties, despite having parents called Higgins and McCormick, answered Scottish to the question and was totally unaware of her Irish antecedents. One teenage girl, though aware that she had people who originated in Ireland called Flood and Devlin, also reported Scottish to the ethnicity question.

Despite many Irish names in the 'Old Town', and in fact, in spite of the symbolism of Irish world cup tee-shirts, an Irish international jersey, and the playing of the Irish nationalist songs of the Wolfe Tones group, noticeable on two separate visits to this area, an articulate Irishness seemed difficult to find. Even with Irish names, like McMenamin, McGuire and McGuigan, answers such as, 'don't know about Irish people', and 'don't know' were common. Indeed, one young family visited had some idea of their Irishness (yet answered Scottish to the ethnic question) in that they had two children called Sean and Siobhan. Nonetheless, in answer to questions concerning that family's background, 'don't know, mother was a Feeney', was as much as the author could entice.

Much of the confusion over ethnicity was even more apparent in the responses of the Holy Cross pupils. In many countries an awareness of one's family's previous generations seems an intrinsic part of the culture of identity. However, given the answers from the young people of the parish it is not an important aspect of culture in St Mary's. Although Duffin wrote Irish-Scottish to the survey question, the interview revealed his mother's family was from Dundalk and his father's side was also from Ireland, though he did not know where. Coyle wrote Irish but had no idea of where in Ireland his people originated or when they came over to Scotland. Quigley also wrote Irish but could only elaborate by saying, 'near the south'. Fitzpatrick had no answer to the inquiry, though she wrote British to the survey question.

One young respondent called Shevlin, answered Scottish to the survey question. On further questioning he did in fact know of some of his people who had come from Ireland. An attempt by the author to open up the question further was met with the answer, 'I've not really thought about it'. Another girl called McKenna also reported 'Scottish' in the questionnaire. After some prompting she expanded on her first answer. 'I wrote Scottish because my parents were born here and my Gran's Scottish and all that . . . My Gran's dad came from Dundalk and I've got relations there'. Possibly one of the most revealing of responses came from a young pupil called Brendan O'Neil. He wrote Irish and Scottish to the survey question, and then informed the author that his grandparents names were O'Neil, McGuire, Brown, and Kelly, an unambiguous Irish lineage. He was unaware, however, of any information relating to his Irish antecedents.

The sense of Irishness varies also in intensity and articulateness. One elderly lady whose grandfathers came from Ireland said, 'I was more Irish fifteen years ago and more distanced now. I think more of the Troubles now than I used to. I have some sympathy with the Unionists and have a more spiritual way of seeing things now'. Another respondent in his fifties reported, 'I'm aware of being Irish for a while, like on St Patrick's Day, maybe a bit of pretence'. Another stated that she was partial to Ireland, 'but I'm Scottish'. A lady with an Irish name forwarded the view that she had 'no real sense of Irishness'.

Some other people mentioned the Troubles in relation to their Irishness. Some people believed that people had forgotten about Ireland because of the Troubles; 'I don't think people are interested. Like Catholics in the Republic, they don't want to know'. For others however, 'in some cases some people don't want to know it. It's also making some people stronger in their Irishness. The suppression and oppression has created a solidarity'. One Irish-born respondent agreed with this viewpoint. A younger interviewee in his twenties also stressed this idea: 'I think a lot of Irish Catholics are turned off by IRA violence. Also many Catholics back them too. I think that more identify because of the Troubles'.

One older respondent with a long association with St Mary's argued: 'Yes, my father left Armagh because of the persecution of Catholics. I feel that it is important that my family know their roots but without bigotry'. Another younger interviewee from the 'Old Town' felt that the Troubles had affected the Irishness of Catholics in Scotland in a number of different ways: 'It divides our opinions. I believe there is a cause to fight for, for a united Ireland. Don't say my name'.

McConnell argues that, 'an obvious factor in the maintenance of [Irish] identity is visiting Ireland'. His survey of second, third, and some fourth generation Irish in Britain revealed that 'two thirds of respondents have visited Ireland as against a fifth of the general population'; with more having 'visited Northern Ireland than population proportions between the two parts of the island would suggest but those who say they have visited Northern Ireland or both parts of the island tend disproportionately to come from Scotland and Northern England'.[37]

In relation to visiting Ireland, the St Mary's results are very similar to those of McConnell's survey. Indeed, 76 per cent of St Mary's parishioners have visited Ireland. When this figure is controlled for age we find the following: almost 60 per cent of those under the age of 24 have visited Ireland, slightly over 70 per cent of those in the age bracket 25 to 34, a similar figure for those aged between 35 and 44, almost 90 per cent of those in the 45 to 54 age-group, all of those aged between 55 and 64, and four in five of those who were over 65 years of age. If we consider that only a fifth of the general population have visited Ireland and that if we hold that a visit to Ireland is related to the maintenance of identity for those of an Irish background, then clearly this feature of the St Mary's parishioners is partly a manifestation of their Irish identity.

In terms of where in Ireland the respondents frequented, some had visited relations, but many were unspecific in their answers. All over Ireland, pilgrimages, holidays, and touring were among the most common responses of those who came into this category. For others though, all six counties of Northern Ireland had been visited as well as having been passed through by those parishioners who visited Donegal. Fourteen counties were mentioned as having been visited in the Republic of Ireland, with Cork being popular. In terms of those who specified where in Ireland they had been, Dublin was the most popular destination.

General Opinions and Attitudes

Those who were subject to the questionnaire were also asked to express their opinion on any topic which had a contemporary Catholic bearing—local, national, or international. Many parishioners had a number of positive remarks to make concerning the current St Mary's parish priest, Monsignor Alexander Devanny. He was clearly viewed as a priest who worked hard and who had 'a down-to-earth attitude'. A number of parish members believed that, like other priests, the local parish priest was overburdened with work, often due to the general lack of priests but also to a diminishing effort on the part of the laity to assist. In fact, this was inhibiting their work as priests, said one churchgoer in his fifties. Others argued that visiting by priests had unfortunately become a thing of the past. A number of the community felt that there had been a positive development in that people could now communicate with priests today, something that was more difficult in years gone by.

Although the contemporary media in Britain is often viewed as unsympathetic to the present Pope, and argue that he is out of line with most of today's Roman Catholics, he remains popular with the Catholics of St Mary's. Some antagonism was shown towards him, one lady stating that she did not like the Pope, feeling he 'was a very hard man and distant from the people'. Nonetheless, comment made about him was often favourable: 'I don't agree with everything the Pope says but will obey because it's the system'. An 'Old Town' resident in his thirties believed that, 'the media turns round what the Pope says'. One parishioner in her seventies backed the Pope: 'It's a strong line, but he's aware of evil in the world'.

Some older parishioners yearned for a few of the old ways, for example, the Latin Mass. Yet younger and middle-aged members of the community felt this change was for the better. A recurrent theme among a number of the churchgoers was the idea that people were losing their sense of sin. A seventy-three-year-old respondent stated, 'There is not the same awareness of sin today. People do things and don't think it is a sin ... priests don't preach about sin now'. Other older members of the community were concerned over the moral standards of the young. One teenager suggested that 'I think the Church is dying out a bit. It is more lenient. Young people don't seem concerned with their religion. Most people go every other Sunday. They don't know about confession before returning to mass. People at school are not very knowledgeable about their religion'.

A young woman from the 'Old Town' opined that 'the faith has lost its unity. Too many priests have too many opinions. One priest will tell you one thing and another another thing. Even in confession you can be told different things. It's confusing on contraception: one says take the pill and another says don't'. A woman churchgoer in her seventies mixed realism with optimism: 'The Church has lost its way because of a lack of Catechism over the years. Teachers not wanting to teach religion has been a big problem. There's still a lot of good people around though, especially among the young'.

For the Holy Cross pupils, much of the focus for this question related to religious education at school. As already stated, most of them based their like or dislike on the quality of the teacher. 'RE in school is good', 'RE is fine. It depends on the teacher. It can be a good period and we can talk open about it'. 'RE is boring at school, because the way the teacher is. It doesn't seem like RE but a history lesson'. 'RE is interesting. I want to take RE at higher. Discussions are good and the teacher explaining parts of the mass is good'. 'RE in school is not good. They don't give you what you want to talk about. It's often regarded as a free period'. 'RE is often a free period, it depends what teacher you get'. 'RE is good, discuss issues that affect us like abortion and understand the faith better as individuals'. 'It's fine, because it teaches you different things, why people have abortion and things. Helps you understand the faith'. 'RE, I just enjoy it'. 'RE is alright, could be better. People who have choices and problems should come in and talk to us'. 'It's pointless really, we don't learn anything that's really useful. All we do is look up Bibles and stuff. They should stop going on about what's wrong and give both sides'.

Many themes were recurrent to young and old members of the St Mary's community. Although they have a number of complaints and grievances, the overall attitude of the parishioners was that they regarded their faith in a positive manner. It was generally regarded that the faith was 'fighting a losing battle', but that there were a number of affirmative features which gave succour to the church-attending respondents.

Conclusion

Overall, it is very important to remember that the vast majority of respondents were church-attenders and their answers were therefore determined from corresponding perspectives. Nonetheless, the survey should be viewed as being representative of 'at very least' half of the parishioners. Although many Catholics in Scotland are currently non- or infrequent church attenders, they still broadly share a social and political identity (though probably a slowly diminishing one). St Mary's parishioners are slightly more Scottish-minded than other Catholics surveyed, but not dramatically so. The investigations allowed the interviewer to probe these questions in greater depth. Although St Mary's active church-attending community have a largely middle class profile in terms of education and employment, there is little other evidence to state that they are significantly different from the majority of Catholic parishioners in the west central belt in their attitudes. The comparisons with the 1990 survey reflect this. Therefore, although they have some differing features, they can be taken as a quite typical parish in terms of overall identity.

That the Catholic community in Scotland, as reflected in the profile of the St Mary's parishioners, remain a distinct ethnic grouping in Scotland, is undoubted. They are now the biggest single church-attending denomination in Scotland. Many of their attitudes permeate the varying ages within their community. On the whole, they believe that the legacy of sectarian discrimination against them in the workplace is still present in Scottish society.

They retain their own educational attributes within the state system. Among other things, this gives them a differing moral and sometimes political character, even agenda. They are strongly against abortion, and at least in terms of the St Mary's church-attenders, they are firmly behind the concept of Catholic schools. Educationally, they compare favourably (at least) with the rest of the community of Scotland. Indeed, it could be argued that the St Mary's active parishioners are a much better educated group than most communities in Scotland, Protestant, Catholic, or otherwise.

The Irish Catholic identity in Scotland today is a complex one. Catholics in Scotland have an identity in relation to both Ireland and Scotland which varies in intensity and emphasis depending on circumstance and environment. 'Irishness' has, for a large number of people, become privatised, and is reduced in many cases to support for Celtic, St Patrick's celebrations, calling children by Irish forenames, and retaining suppressed political feelings on political relations between Ireland and Britain. The formative influences of the Irish identity have changed. Part of the reason for this however, is that there exist few structured means of expressing 'Irishness'. There are few vehicles of expression adequate to its self-consciousness. The experience of many decades of education which has neglected to consider the history of the Catholic people of Scotland, or indeed, of the historic relationship between Ireland and Britain, and which has constantly emphasised one identity, i.e., a common Scottish and British one, has been guaranteed to dilute the Irishness of that community.

This community can be either Irish or Scottish in certain settings, but on the whole its members find it difficult to define and articulate their identity. Irish Catholics in Scotland today can possess more than one identity and even several layers of identity. On the whole, the Irish of St Mary's retain a fluctuating and multi-dimensional identity. Irish identity in Scotland has been shaped by the immigrants' experiences. Many of the Irish, like immigrants in other countries, thought the best way to survive was to keep a low profile.

The overall survey material shows that although most

church-going Catholics believe their roots to be Irish, a high proportion of them reported their heritage as Scottish. Identity itself can often be a source of confusion, inconsistency, and even anxiety. Individuals may find it difficult to define the content and origins of their identity. Bearing in mind the loss of identity inevitable via incorporation into the host society, the inability or desire not to articulate an Irish background should be seen mainly as a result of anti-Catholicism in Scotland as well as the consequence of exposure to a dominating and antagonistic indigenous culture and identity. But also, it is the result of Scotland/Britain's relationship with Ireland over a period of hundreds of years.

Although the concept of ethnicity applies to the Irish in Scotland, it must be remembered that few communities are completely watertight. Indeed, the evidence here shows that the Irish and Catholic community, as well as being a distinctive one, is also splintering. This reflects in a lessening Church commitment and a loss, or contraction, of an articulate Irish identity.

Despite confusion over the question of identity, it may be the case that the greatest single challenge to the Catholics of St Mary's and of Catholics in Scotland in general (and indeed for concerned Christian's everywhere), is their struggle against a secular society, which promises a very different world from the one which we all presently inhabit.

References

1. See J.F. McCaffrey, 'Politics and the Catholic Community Since 1878,' in D. McRoberts *Modern Scottish Catholicism, 1878–1978*, (Glasgow, 1979), pp. 140–155.

2. See T. Gallagher, 'Catholics in Scottish Politics', *Bulletin of Scottish Politics*, I, 2.

3. J.F. McCaffrey, 'Roman Catholics in Scotland in the nineteenth and twentieth centuries,' *Records of The Scottish Church History Society*, 1983, 21, 2.

4. J. Brand, *The National Movement in Scotland*, (London 1978).

5. W.L. Miller, *The End of British Politics: Scottish and English Political Behaviour in the seventies*, (Oxford, 1981), pp. 144–6.

6. See results of 1990 survey in J.M. Bradley, *Ethnic and Religious Identity in Modern Scotland* (Avebury, Aldershot, 1995).

7. See example in *The Herald*, 9/2/95.

8. See J.M. Bradley, *Ethnic and Religious Identity in Modern Scotland*, (Avebury, Aldershot, 1995).

9. *Flourish*, May 1991.

10. Wolfe was in fact removed from the Party hierarchy because of this outburst.

11. For example, see interview with Ian Davidson, Chairman of Strathclyde Region's Educational Committee, in *Flourish*, May, 1991.

12. *Times Higher Educational Supplement for Scotland*, 14/6/85.

13. *Evening Times*, 6/6/85.

14. *Flourish*, July 1991.

15. Jimmy Wray, Glasgow Provan, stated, 'I hope that people will vote for the Party they want to vote for . . . the Roman Catholic Church should not be able to dictate who they should vote for'. *Herald*, 5/7/91.

16. Interview with the then Archbishop Winning, 5/7/91.

17. Interview with Father Noel Barry, editor of *Flourish*, 17/7/91.

18. Interview with Archbishop Winning and Noel Barry. A number of Catholic Labour MPs contacted the Flourish office to give their support to the Archbishop.

19. *Herald*, 5/7/91.

20. See *Herald*, 8/7/91, article by Brian Meek.

21. *Herald*, 7/7/91.

22. *Flourish*, March 1989.

23. *Flourish*, May 1988.

24. *Flourish*, May 1990.

25. See *Flourish*, 29/4/89, for the results of Gallup Poll which considered such questions among Catholics.

26. *Herald*, 11/7/91.

27. *Scottish Catholic Observer*, 19/7/91.

28. See Tom Gallagher, *Glasgow, The Uneasy Peace* (Manchester 1987) and T.M. Devine (ed), *Irish Immigrants and Scottish Society in the Nineteenth and Twentieth Centuries, Proceedings of the Scottish historical studies seminar, University of Strathclyde*, (Edinburgh, 1990).

29. See Bradley, *Ethnic and Religious Identity*.

30. *Scottish Catholic Observer*, 19/10/90.

31. *Ibid.*, 2/11/90.

32. *Ibid.*, 16/11/90.

33. See Bradley, *Ethnic and Religious Identity*. Also, T. Campbell and P. Woods, *The Glory and the Dream, The History of Celtic F.C., 1987–1986*, (Edinburgh, 1986).

34. See M. Hickman, '*A study of the incorporation of the Irish in Britain with special reference to Catholic state education; involving a comparison of the attitudes of pupils and teachers in selected Catholic schools in London and Liverpool*,' Ph.D., University of London, 1990, also, L. Curtis, *Nothing But The Same Old Story: The Roots of Anti-Irish Racism*, (5th edition, 1988).

35. The Northern Ireland conflict has also encouraged Catholics to maintain a low profile, see Bradley, *Ethnic and Religious Identity*.

36. Hickman, 'Incorporation of the Irish in Britain', p. 170.

37. See Professor James McConnell's survey reported in *The Irish Post*, weekly from October 29th 1994 to February 4th 1995.

CHAPTER 7

The Italian Community

Joseph M. Bradley

This chapter will look at the Italian community of St Mary's and its environs. Over two dozen of the present and recent Italians of St Mary's were either interviewed by the writer or completed a questionnaire, described in Chapter 5, which was a variant of that constructed for other members of the parish. Although some of the text will refer to specifically Italian matters, other parts will simply compare attitudes of those of Italian origin with 'other' parishioners. The notes will fall into three parts: brief reference to the Italians generally, results of the survey, and anecdotal material arising from interviews in relation to the experiences of some individual Italian families connected with St Mary's parish.

Context

Although some work has been carried out on Scotland's Italian communities, generally few people know much about them. Perceptions are dominated by ideas about Italians owning chip shops, making ice cream, as well as involving Mafia stereotypes. According to Colpi, there are some 250,000 Italians in Britain with less than ten per cent, around 23,000, resident in Scotland.[1] This community is made up of people born in Italy or of Italian parentage, grandparents etc.

As one of the primary Catholic countries of Europe much of Italian identity was built on aspects of Catholic culture. Although Colpi seems to refer to their lack of piety, popularly, Catholicism remains one of the characteristics of 'being Italian'.

As far as St Mary's is concerned there is evidence of an Italian community from at least the latter part of the 19th century. The vast majority of the 'Italians' of the parish appear to have their origins in southern Italy. Indeed, many can trace their roots to towns and villages which lie within a fifty-mile radius south of Rome, particularly the areas around Lazio and Campobasso. In fact, only three St Mary's respondents to the questionnaire did not come from these areas.

Chain migration has also been a hallmark of the Italians, whereby certain sources developed links with certain destinations and communities. This meant that it became common for migrants who chose to come to Scotland, to settle in areas which were already inhabited by people to whom they could relate. It seems likely that most people who departed Italy were economic migrants, driven by a desire for a better way of life and opposed to the subsistence agriculture they were used to. Every respondent to the questionnaire stressed that their family had left Italy for precisely this reason.

Profile and Attitudes

Over fifty per cent of respondents stated that their families knew someone in Scotland when they themselves arrived; almost half of them already had family in place. Almost all came directly to Scotland, three families arriving via France and another from England. Some of the present parishioners of the Italian community had family who had arrived in the 1890s; a substantial number came either before World War One and some during the War. Almost one quarter of the respondents' families came to Scotland after the Second World War.

A majority of the St Mary's Italian respondents were born in Scotland, one was born in France, and one quarter born in Italy itself. Most had Italian-born parents; the French-born respondent also had a French parent, three had parents from a Scottish background, while two had an Irish lineage. All respondents had Catholic parents apart from one who had a non-Catholic father. All married respondents had married a Catholic, except two who had married members of the Church of Scotland, but who had since converted to Catholic.

There is a popular perception of the Italians being

self-employed on arrival in Scotland, particularly in the fish-and-chip-shop and ice-cream trades. Certainly the business side of the perception holds for many Italians of St Mary's. Half of the respondents in fact had started their own business in the area; another quarter worked with relations in their business (see below).

With reference to education the Italians do not appear at first sight to be as well educated as the majority of the St Mary's community. Twenty-nine per cent of them had acquired a degree and three others had attained highers. However, these figures must be viewed in the context of the age of many of the respondents, forty-three per cent of whom were over sixty-five years of age. In addition, many Italians pursued a livelihood within the family business and this would have been a barrier to viewing education as a means for social progress. Indeed, in some cases, time-consuming education may have proved an obstacle to a progressive family business.

The chapter on the wider experience in employment refers to traditional discrimination against Catholics. Much of this discrimination had traditionally evolved or has been manifest through the identifying of religious identity from a person's Irish name and/or the Catholic school they attended. The questionnaire results show that the perception of the Italian community corresponds to that of the traditional Irish one. Three-quarters of respondents believed that Catholics would be discriminated against in favour of Protestants in the workplace; a quarter of these recorded their own experiences. Only four respondents replied negatively to this question.

Politically, the Italians seemed slightly less inclined to politics than their Catholic neighbours or the wider community. Despite some typical immigrant experiences, their political history as an immigrant group is quite different from that of the Irish, who were also of course a much larger body. However, like other Catholics they do favour the Labour Party more than any other party, almost half of them doing so. Nonetheless, close to half are indifferent to political parties, not favouring any one in particular. Two respondents favoured the Conservatives.

With reference to the issue of the future constitutional position of Scotland within the United Kingdom, only one respondent viewed independence as desirable. Another three parishioners believed things should remain as they are. The most popular Italian feeling in terms of this question was to stay within the United Kingdom; almost two in five believing an Assembly would work for Scotland and the same number supporting the idea of Scotland being better understood by the Government of the day.

A majority of the Italians surveyed were regular church-attenders. In terms of attitudes to crucial 'Catholic' questions of the day, the Italians are similar to other St Mary's parishioners. Only ten per cent of respondents were against the retention of Catholic schools in Scotland; all others being very strongly or fairly strongly in their favour. All respondents were strongly against abortion.

Identity

Chapter 5 referred to the custom of visiting Ireland as being a marker of Irish identity for the majority of Catholics in Scotland. If we apply the same thinking to the Italians of Hamilton, then we clearly see that it is also an indication of identity for them. Regardless of which generation of Italian the respondent was, all had visited Italy; two-thirds of them had visited very often. All others had visited the country occasionally or sometimes (apart from one who had only been once).

The Italian identity is furthered strengthened in relation to the country's language. Only one person could speak no Italian (which may be related to the family being of mixed-Italian/Scots-origin and having arrived in Hamilton around 1900). All those who could speak fluent Italian were born there. However, all other respondents were able to speak a little of the language or a few words – a clear indicator of Italian identity.

Although Scotland has become a multi-cultural society, there often appears to be little mainstream recognition of identities other than Scottish or British ones. This is most clearly manifest in relation to Irish identity in Scotland, a matter referred to elsewhere.[2] Nonetheless, how do the Italian community view themselves? Every respondent to the questionnaire acknowledged, and indeed appeared to be proud of their 'Italianness'. Despite Larkhall, Glasgow, and Hamilton being the birthplace of some parishioners, one quarter identified themselves as Italian. One respondent saw himself as French/Italian and another as Irish-Italian. The majority of those subject to the questionnaire however viewed themselves as Scots-Italian. Clearly, these results reflect the Italian identity as a very strong one amongst first, second, and third generation Italians. Nonetheless, like the Irish identity for some parishioners, and indeed for other Catholics in Scotland, there is often a lack of clarity in these identities.

One of the interviewees for this chapter had a background in the Portella (near Cassino) area of Italy. The Di Mambro family arrived in Scotland around 1919 and came to St Mary's parish about 1926/27. The family rented a local café and eventually involved themselves in ice-cream wholesale.

The original family had neither the time nor the money to return home, but as the business developed the children were able to go back and visit relations. Their son, Gaetano, married a local girl (Raziantonia) whose mother had come from Italy and whose grandparents on her father's side had also originated there.

The grandchildren of the original Di Mambros prove an interesting case in assessing contemporary Italian identity. A sense of their heritage is maintained by way of their forenames; all have Italian names, and all are conscious of their 'Italianness'. They are Anna Maria, Giovanni (John), Francesco, Alessandra Lucia, Paolino, and Carla. Trips to Italy have been a feature of family life for many years, and indeed some have spent periods of months in Italy. John is one such example and at one stage spent three months in Milan.

Both Anna Maria and John consider themselves to be Scots-Italian. However, John's identity reflects the experience of some of the second and third generation Irish of Scotland. He finds himself between countries. In fact, he recognises that he has no Scottish or British heritage, and feels no affinity with things Scottish. Nonetheless, he also recognises that when he goes to Italy he is identified as Scottish, though more discerning Italians would recognise that he is not 'simply' Scottish. John carries two passports.

Although he was always an active Italian, in that he was involved in the Casa d'Italia (House of Italy) club in Glasgow in the 1970s and 1980s, unlike many Italians, he was never particularly interested in football. However, when Italy did so well in the 1990 World Cup tournament, John found it expedient to drive to Glasgow and join in the celebrations of flying flags and tooting car horns that took place in the city's George Square. Again, as for many Irish in Scotland, football became a symbol of John's Italian identity and a medium for its celebration.[3]

'Other' Experiences

The Picozzi family are only one example of the 'chip-shop' culture of many Italians in Scotland. Nicandro Picozzi moved from Italy (near Venafro) to Scotland in the early 1900s, settling first in Airdrie and then in Hamilton (1927). By this time Nicandro had married a local girl (Agnes Devlin, of Irish immigrant stock), and they had six children, all called by Italian names. Two of the children, Nicandro and Vincenzo, returned to Italy to become priests (they still live there). Indeed, Vincenzo assisted the famous Father O'Flaherty who helped many Jews escape from Rome and certain fate if they were captured by the Nazis during the War.

Locally, the family opened a fish-and-chip shop in Chapel Street in Hamilton. Two of the offspring of Nicandro and Agnes now live in Birmingham, one stays in Airdrie, while Maria Luisa is now a member of the nearby St Anne's parish.

The Graziani family also had a deep connection with St Mary's. Amerigo was born in 1890 in Pescaglia, near Lucca in Northern Italy. He came to Scotland in 1900 and in 1917 he married his Italian-born fiancée in St John's Church, Uddingston. Again a family business situated at the rear of the Odeon Cinema, but eventually settling in Castle Street, provided the family income. Amerigo and Candida had seven children; one of their grandchildren remains a nun with the Poor Clares in nearby Blantyre. All of the original Graziani children were baptised and educated in St Mary's parish. Amerigo died in 1952, his wife in 1982.

The Fraioli family were parishioners who also managed their own business. In 1920, Giovanni (John) Fraioli opened The Continental Restaurant at Hamilton's Old Cross. Although the family are of the belief that they were the first Italians to bring a chef from Italy, they also had to re-arrange their Italian menu to suit the then tastes of the locals. Today, the Fraiolis are still remembered in the town for their ice cream.

Another family who involved themselves in the ice-cream business, were the Capaldis. Ernest was born in 1901 in Filignano in the province of Isernia in southern Italy. He came to this country in 1923 to work with his brother, Giuliano, who lived in Cleland. In 1927 Ernest married Emily Pacitti who then lived in Carfin. They had a café with a flat above it in Chapel Street. During the summer, Ernest took to the streets to sell ice cream from a wheelbarrow while his wife looked after the shop.

Their only son, Mario, was baptised in St Mary's in 1923. He also married an Italian girl called Maria Paccitti. They reside in Edelwood in Hamilton. Ernest's brother Giuliano, whom he originally came to Scotland to work for early in the century, now lives in Lochgelly, Fife, aged 92.

One of the experiences of the Capaldi family in emigrating to Scotland was a common one for many Italians. In fact the experience of being an alien living in a country at war was a negative one.

On 10 June 1940, Mussolini joined forces with Hitler. As a result, Scotland and Britain were at war with Italy, and this, not unexpectedly, affected existing perceptions of Italians in Scotland. Italians who had worked hard in Scotland for many years and had contributed to economic life here now became targets for those who were less than rational in their actions. Many Italian businesses were looted and ransacked and 'Tallies' became the object of violence.

The story of St Mary's Italian parishioners like the Di Marco family is an example of what many innocent Italians had to suffer. Angie Di Marco was a young girl at the time. Her family owned the Monte Carlo café in the centre of Hamilton. Angie recounts the story herself:

> There was an awful feeling of something about to happen. One or two regular customers came in and said there was a gang going round smashing shop windows. We heard the smashing of glass at the Cross Cafe. Then we heard D'Ambrosio's windows being smashed and the shouting. I was ushered out through the back with my mother and two sisters, but my father wouldn't come. Outside a crowd of women waited as they were all shouting for blood. However, some customers protected us and we ran upstairs to our flat. Before we got there, Mrs Brownlee, our neighbour, opened her door and took us in. When my father came up he looked whitewashed. He said, 'Twelve years work gone in twelve minutes'. Mrs Brownlee had just made him a cup of tea when four policemen came to arrest him. My mother said, 'Take a good look at your daddy. You'll never see him again'. We never did.[4]

These events were utterly condemned by the priests at St Mary's, particularly by Fathers Kilcoyne and O'Sullivan. Angie's father was one of over a thousand internees who were being shipped to Canada when their boat, the *Arandora Star*, was torpedoed off the west coast of Ireland by a German U-boat. Hundreds of Italian lives were lost in the disaster of July 1940, including three local Hamilton men, Silvestro D'Ambrosio, Guiseppe Delgrosso, and Mariano Di Marco. A generation before, Mariano Di Marco had fought for Italy against Germany; he had been in Scotland for twenty-two years.[3] His family remain parishioners of St Mary's parish. The experience of being interned during the Second World War was shared by a number of local Italians.

One of the most significant Italian contributions to the Hamilton area originates with the Martalo family. Luigi Martalo was born in 1927 in Lecce, near Brindisi, in the south-east of the country. Luigi married Rita Pisano from Treviso near Venezia, in the more prosperous northern part of the country. On seeing an advert in Venice for couples to emigrate, they both embarked for Scotland. After husband and wife worked as a chauffeur and cook for two and a half years for the Hamilton industrialist, John Graham, they moved to Ayr to work.

Luigi decided he would start his own business back in Hamilton. In less than three years he opened seven fish-and-chip shops, and eventually thirteen of them. He believes the fact that they were much cleaner than the existing ones in the area, and that he offered a more extensive menu (including pizzas and chicken suppers), was his key to success. Around 1967, Luigi bought the Grange Hotel and had it re-open as the Avonbridge. Again, he introduced the novelty of dinner dances, which proved successful. In the early 1970s he purchased the Bothwell Bridge Hotel. He also opened local restaurants, including the Quovadis Ristorante.

One of the most important results of the Martalo presence in Hamilton has been his ability as a facilitator for other Italians wishing to immigrate. Luigi reckons that in his first ten years in the area, he brought over thirty to thirty-five other Italians or their families to work for him. Many moved on to work for themselves and to develop other fish-and-chip shops around Lanarkshire. Luigi Martalo now has around 125 people working for him, with approximately one quarter of them from Italy. The Italian connection is maintained with a vast array of Italian produce still being purchased by the Martalos, some even being sold on to other buyers.

The Martalos have three children, Maria, Anna, and Diana, who were all baptised in St Mary's. Likewise, all three married fellow Italians in St Mary's Church – two into the Armando family and one to a Capaldi. Luigi and Rita have three grandchildren, also called by Italian names, Gianni, Luca, and Daniele. For the Martalo family, the St Mary's connection has always been a strong one.

The Italian influence on St Mary's and indeed in the Hamilton area generally has been a significant one. Although all of those who came into the bracket of being Italian and who were interviewed for this chapter stressed how happy they were in the area and with the friendships they had developed, clearly they also had a great affinity with the heritage and culture of their country of origin. Their identities took more meaning for them and their place in society was better expressed within the context of being Italian in a Scottish setting.

References

1. T. Colpi, 'The Scottish Italian Community: senza un campanile?' *The Innes Review*, Vol XLIV, No. 2, Autumn 1993, pp. 153–67.

2. See J.M. Bradley, *Ethnic and Religious Identity in Modern Scotland* (Avebury, Aldershot, 1995).

3. *Ibid.*

4. A.M. Di Mambro, article in *The Sunday Times, Scotland*, p. 5, 'Welcome home for Italian enterprise', 7/7/91.

5. *The Hamilton Advertiser*, 13/7/40.

Obituaries of St Mary's Parish Priests

These edited obituaries first appeared in the *Catholic Directory for Scotland*.

Very Rev. Michael Condon (d. 1902)

The death of this venerable and saintly priest, the doyen of the Glasgow clergy, removes from our midst a loveable personality, and breaks an interesting link with the past history of Glasgow Catholicity. Up till a few years before his death he had been in active work, and his extensive labours during more than half a century had left their mark, not only in Glasgow, but in other parts of the old Western Vicariate.

He was born at Craves, Coolcappa, Co. Limerick, on 23 September 1817. Feeling called to the ecclesiastical state, he entered St Mary's Missionary College, Youghal, in 1841, completing his studies at All Hallows, Dublin, which he entered in 1845. He was ordained sub-deacon by Bishop Walsh of Nova Scotia on 8 March 1845, and deacon by Archbishop Murray of Dublin on 19 September following. Coming to Scotland immediately after he was raised to the priesthood by Bishop Murdoch on 6 October of the same year, he was immediately appointed assistant at St Mary's, Glasgow. His labours lay chiefly among the poorest classes of his own countrymen, who at the time were making large immigrations into the country. Like so many of his colleagues of that day who laboured so assiduously in the fever-tainted districts of the city, he fell a victim to the contagion, and for a time his life was despaired of. Even when in good health his slender frame and clear and delicate complexion gave little promise of the long life that lay before him. On recovering from this illness he was, in the summer of 1847, transferred to the distant charge of Campbeltown. His two years' stay at this place was marked by the building of a church, towards the expenses of which he himself gathered £900. In May 1849, came his appointment to Hamilton. His labours in this mission are described as Herculean, ministering as he did single-handed for many years, to a widely scattered and rapidly increasing population, besides having to cope with a huge debt and many other difficulties. But his quiet activity and methodical ways made all smooth. In 1859 he was sent to form the new mission of St Lawrence's, Greenock. In this charge he remained for fifteen years, and his long residence was marked by the extinction of debt, the purchase of properties to serve as presbytery and convent, the establishment of a Catholic cemetery, and the erection of new schools. Such successful labours in the missionary field did not pass unnoticed by his ecclesiastical superiors, and when the Glasgow Chapter was formed in 1884, he was chosen by Archbishop Eyre to be one of the first Canons. The following year he was invited to take charge of St Patrick's, Glasgow. With his wonted energy he proceeded to wipe out the debt remaining on the old church, and in the course of a few years he succeeded in doing so. Even in extreme old age his zeal and courage for high enterprises did not desert him. On the eve of celebrating the golden jubilee of his priesthood he set about the task of rebuilding the church and schools of St Patrick's – a formidable undertaking from which even a younger man might well shrink. He was, however, shortly afterwards, owing to his increasing infirmity, relieved of the main burden of his responsibilities by the appointment of an Administrator; but to the end he took an immense interest in the welfare of both schools and church.

The fruitfulness of his missionary exertions was due in no small part to his methodical habits. Perhaps that also was the secret of his long life after the endurance of so many arduous and trying experiences. Order was his first rule. The routine of his daily life – his spiritual exercise, services in church, visitation of his flock and schools, organisation of the various parochial activities – all went like clockwork. It was his practice for many years to make an annual house-to-house census of his people. His parochial accounts and the record of his various financial transactions were models of order and accuracy. He was most scrupulous in attending to his correspondence. Every letter he received was carefully preserved with its answer endorsed. His few hours of leisure snatched from so busy a life were devoted to the study of ecclesiastical antiquities, particularly ancient ruins; and he was an authority on the past condition and statistics of the Catholic Church in Scotland. He has left behind him in manuscript several volumes of historical researches, which it is hoped will one day see the light. He was endowed with a well-cultivated mind, provided with rich stores of knowledge, which a singularly retentive memory could immediately recall as occasion required. This, added to his gentle and sympathetic nature, made him a sage and prudent counsellor, much valued and sought after by his brother clergy.

For several years after his retirement from active duty, though, of course, pressed down with the weakness and weight of years, Canon Condon enjoyed comparatively good health, and took an active interest in all that went on about him. So far as possible, he was most regular in attending the monthly Canons' meeting. Even in the spring of last year he was able to assist at the funerals of Archbishop Eyre and Canon Carmichael. A few days before his death he was prostrated by a chill, which rapidly assumed alarming symptoms. The last Rites were administered by the Rev. Dr Mullin. For a time he seemed to rally somewhat; but the end came peacefully at last on the morning of Tuesday, 17 June.

Very Rev. James Canon Danaher (d. 1886)

This widely-known and esteemed clergyman was born at Croom, in the County of Limerick, in 1821, and was one of four sons whom his pious parents gave to the service of the altar. To prepare himself for the ecclesiastical state, which he had early resolved to embrace, he spent some years at St Mary's College, Youghal, after which he entered the Missionary College of All Hallows and there completed the usual course of studies. Having given his services to the Western District of Scotland, he was ordained priest by Bishop Murdoch on the 6th June, 1845. He began his long and meritorious career of missionary labour at St Andrew's, Glasgow, whence after a few months he was transferred to Greenock as assistant priest. Two years later, on the death of the Rev. Richard Sinnott, he succeeded to the charge of the mission, and held this post for the next five years. At that time the Catholic population of Greenock was computed to be about 6000, and for this large number there was only one church and one day and evening school. He at once set about raising funds to build an additional church, but he had not yet been able to accomplish this when the time of his removal came. In his endeavours to supply the educational wants of his people he met with signal success, for before the close of 1850 no less than seven day and night schools were in full operation. One of these – a 'Ragged School' – having a daily average attendance of 150 children, was started by him to counteract the insidious efforts of proselytisers, whose exertions among the destitute Catholics in our large towns were at that time particularly systematic and mischievous. In the cause of the poor of his flock he engaged in 1850 in a determined struggle with the Greenock Parochial Board, which insisted on bringing up in Protestantism the children of Catholic parents; and the vigorous resistance which he made to this injustice attracted much attention. Shortly after this the fierce passions which were evoked by the 'Papal Aggression' and the passing of the Ecclesiastical Titles Bill exposed Father Danaher to no small risk, and brought into prominence the manly firmness of his character. The bold stand which he made in defence of his people, when a deadly feud arose between the Orangemen and the Catholics connected with the sugar refineries, is not yet forgotten in the West of Scotland. On one occasion, during a 12th of July celebration, his church and presbytery were attacked by a furious Orange mob and much damage was done to both.

In July, 1852, Father Danaher was replaced in Greenock by the late Rev. William Gordon; and after spending a few months at St Andrew's, Glasgow, and Dumbarton, he was appointed in October to the charge of the recently-erected church of St Joseph's, Glasgow. During a considerable part of the seven years that he passed in this populous and important mission, the scarcity of priests was so great in the Western District that he had to work it single-handed. He found it fairly well provided with schools; but as they did not come up to the high standard which he, a life-long enthusiast in all that concerned education, always kept before him, he erected new school buildings shortly before his connection with it was severed. His solicitude for the more necessitous part of his parishioners impelled him from the very outset to rent a large hall, where 130 poor children were educated gratuitously. In 1859 St Joseph's passed into the hands of the Jesuit Fathers, and Father Danaher was transferred to Hamilton.

A great change, from an ecclesiastical point of view, came over the wide district to which he was now called during the twenty-seven years of his incumbency. The Catholic body, owing to the large development of local works, increased enormously in various places; and many independent missions were from time to time carved out of the tract of country which was then committed to his care. It will readily be perceived that while this rapid growth in the numbers of his flock was going on, and before other priests were sent to relieve him of part of his responsibility, his work was trying and laborious in no small degree. In Hamilton itself, to which his sphere of duty was in course of time restricted, he left material proofs of his zeal in the great improvement of the church, and above all in the excellent schools with which he enriched it. For ten years he was a valued and most efficient member of the Burgh School Board. All classes of the community held him in the greatest respect, and it is said that no one was more universally popular. He had great gifts of nature and character to attract men and to retain their affection and esteem, and amongst them a fine presence, great suavity and frankness, and a gentlemanly bearing. As a preacher, and as a public speaker on any subject which claimed his advocacy, whether religious or social or political, his reputation stood very high.

In the beginning of 1884 Father Danaher was appointed one of the Canons in the newly-erected Chapter of the Archdiocese of Glasgow. He had for a number of years before this held some of the chief offices to which his clerical brethren could appoint him, and had taken a prominent part in their business matters. His healthy and robust appearance gave promise of a long and vigorous old age; and even in the autumn of 1886, when certain symptoms caused anxiety to his friends, and an assistant priest was sent to enable him to take the rest which his physician prescribed, there was little or nothing to indicate that the end was near at hand. On the afternoon of Saturday, the 13th November, he had just returned from a drive into the country, during which he had been particularly bright and cheerful, and sat down at the fire, when without the least warning he suddenly expired. *Angina pectoris* was the cause of death.

Next evening the corpse was removed to the church, which was visited during the whole of Monday by crowds of his sorrowing flock. The funeral service took place on the following Tuesday in St Mary's, Hamilton, and was attended by Archbishop Eyre and a very large number of clergy from different parts of the country. Several Protestant clergymen, the Provost and Sheriff, most of the Magistrates and Town Councillors, and many of the leading people of the town and district, were also present. Solemn Requiem Mass was celebrated by Canon O'Keeffe, and the funeral oration was delivered by Canon Condon, a classmate of the deceased, his predecessor in Hamilton, and very dear friend. 'His Grace then pronounced the absolution at the bier, after which the coffin was borne to the hearse, amid the tears and sobs of hundreds of parishioners who clustered round all that was left of their late pastor, in a manner which evidenced in a large degree the great love that exists between the Irish pastor and his flock. Outside the church, when the coffin was placed in the hearse, was a crowd which must have numbered close on 5000 souls. A battalion of the Highland Light Infantry was drawn up in line on the west side of the church in Cadzow Street, and as the funeral *cortège*, consisting of a hearse and over 30 carriages, passed, the detachment lined both sides of the street. The *cortège* was watched by crowds of onlookers who lined the Bothwell Road for some miles, and not a few walked all the way to Dalbeth, where the remains were interred alongside those of his brother, who was for a considerable time incumbent at Duntocher. Arrived at the cemetery, a procession of priests and mourners, headed by His Grace the Archbishop, was formed; and amid the chanting of the *Benedictus* by the priests, and the tears of many dear friends, the mortal remains of Canon Danaher, covered by innumerable wreaths placed upon his coffin by loving hands, were lowered into the grave. The town bells were tolled by order of the Provost and Magistrates, and the flag above the

Town Hall was half-mast high. The goodwill and esteem in which the Canon was held by every section of the population were abundantly testified by the large number of ladies and gentlemen, of high social position, who thronged the church during the celebration of the services for the dead, and the thousands who filled the streets and lined the route to Dalbeth for many miles. Reference to the sad event was made from the pulpits of two Established churches and one United Presbyterian church, in a manner which showed in a marked way the good feeling which exists, thanks to him that is gone, between Catholics and Protestants in Hamilton.' – (*Glasgow Observer*). We understand that Canon Danaher had arranged that nearly all that he possessed should go to various religious and charitable institutions.

Rev. Peter Donnelly (d. 1903)

The Rev. Peter Donnelly was born in Greenock on 5th July, 1853. He came of a pious Irish stock. Three of his maternal uncles and an older brother were priests and missionaries in the West of Scotland. Manifesting from his earliest years a strong inclination for the priesthood, he was sent in September, 1865, to Rockwell College, Co. Tipperary, Ireland, to begin the long preparation required for the holy state to which he felt called. During his nine years in Rockwell College he distinguished himself greatly in his classes, and secured many coveted prizes. On the opening of the Diocesan College at Partickhill on 5th October, 1874, he was one of the first students to be admitted. He was ordained priest in St Andrew's, Glasgow, by Archbishop Eyre, on 25th June, 1876. Immediately after his ordination, Father Donnelly was appointed assistant priest to the Rev. Edward Noonan, who was in charge of the Sacred Heart Mission, Glasgow. The three years he spent in Bridgeton are still held in grateful remembrance by the people of that district. In June, 1879, he was transferred to St John's, Glasgow, where for over a year he acted as one of the assistants to the Rev. Valentine Chisholm. In May, 1880, he was appointed to the rising, but very struggling, parish of Blantyre. His strenuous labours on behalf of those over whom he had been set in charge were always apparent, and, indeed, so zealous was he amongst his flock that he was stricken down by a virulent fever, and for weeks his life was despaired of. Early in December, 1886, he was appointed to the charge of the mission in Hamilton, in succession to Canon Danaher, then deceased. Here, in Hamilton, he was destined to spend the remainder of his life. In the spring of 1902 Father Donnelly was again stricken down with an illness, and from the very beginning those about his bedside knew full well what the end was to be. He bore his weakness and his suffering with excellent resignation. He did not fear death; he rather dwelt on it. He often spoke of his approaching end and of his funeral arrangements, even to the minutest details, as if life were something in which he had no personal concern. The end came on Thursday, the 20th November, when, in the sentiments of Christian faith and hope, and fortified by the Rites of the Church, he yielded up himself to God.

Rev. William M'Avoy (d. 1932)

The Rev. William M'Avoy was born in Glasgow on 17th March 1862. He entered Blairs College in 1877, went to Douai in 1882, spent one year there and returned home to complete his studies at the old seminary of St Peter's, Partick. He was ordained priest by Archbishop Eyre in St Andrew's Cathedral, Glasgow, on 24th June 1888. After serving for two years on the staff of St John's, Glasgow, he was transferred to St Patrick's, Dumbarton, and remained there till 1896. In that year he received as his first charge the mission of Cadzow. In the words of Canon Mullin, quoted in the *Glasgow Observer*: 'He entered into the lives of the people, sharing their joys and their sorrows, and striving to brighten and uplift the lot of the mining community. In particular at the time of a disastrous strike, when he felt that the poor were unfairly treated and advantage taken of their position, he stood up manfully by his people and helped in a notable degree to bring about a fair solution to the dispute. Ever afterwards the miners of all the surrounding districts realised the friend they had in Fr. M'Avoy and they looked to him as a safe guide and trusted counsellor.' In 1903 Fr. M'Avoy succeeded Fr. Donnelly as parish priest of Hamilton. 'In this wider sphere of labour,' to quote Canon Mullin again, 'Fr. M'Avoy gave further evidence of the zeal and earnestness that had marked him since the day of his ordination. He knew that his work could not be really satisfactory unless done through and for God and so he was unfailing in his daily Mass and all his other spiritual exercises, praying for his flock and for all dear to them and for all their wants both spiritual and temporal. Without any show, nay almost by his gaiety of manner, he was a man of deep piety.' In Hamilton Fr. M'Avoy built the new presbytery, and at the time of his death had collected a considerable sum for the building of a new church. He also added to the existing school buildings in order to cope with the demand for increased accommodation. For many years he served on various public bodies, the Parish Council, School Board and Education Authority. His services were given without stint and were deservedly appreciated by his colleagues.

He collapsed while preparing for Mass on Saturday, 13th August; he was annointed, and died almost immediately. Solemn Requiem was celebrated by Rev. Denis Scannell at St Mary's, Hamilton, on 22nd August. His Grace the Archbishop of Glasgow was represented by the Right Mgr. Rev. Daly, V.G. A. Large number of priests were present and representatives from many public bodies. The absolutions were given by Rev. Denis Scannell. The funeral cortège moved away through crowded streets to Dalbeth Cemetery, where the committal service was read by Mgr. Daly.

Very Rev. Bartholomew Canon Flynn (d. 1949)

The Very Rev. Bartholomew Canon Flynn was born at Springburn, Glasgow, on 12th March, 1877. He received his primary education at the local parochial school and at St Aloysius' College, Glasgow, and entered Blairs College in 1891. From Blairs he passed, in 1894, to the Royal Scots College, Valladolid, where he completed his humanities and studied philosophy. The five years he spent in Spain made a deep impression on his young mind, and he ever after retained the most cherished memories of the *Colegio*. In 1899 he was sent for his course of theology to St Peter's College, New Kilpatrick, and was raised to the priesthood by Archbishop Maguire in St Andrew's Cathedral, Glasgow, on 24th June, 1903. His first curacy was at St Mirin's, Paisley, where he laboured for seven years. In 1910 he was transferred to St Bridget's, Baillieston, in which parish he served for six years. For a short time in 1915 he supplied in St Fillan's, Houston, and he was assistant in Our Lady and St Mark's, Alexandria, when an appeal was made for army chaplains. This was in the darkest days of the First World War; the need for Catholic chaplains was urgent, and Father Flynn was prompt to answer the call. He was gazetted on 16th November, 1916, and was sent immediately to the Belgian Front. Here and in France he served during two strenuous years. At Coxyde, Belgium, in August, 1917, he had the sad consolation of laying to rest the mortal remains of his friend and fellow-chaplain, the beloved Doctor Gordon. After his demobilization in 1919 he served for short periods in several parishes. It was from St Patrick's, Anderston, that he was appointed to the charge of St Mary's, Duntocher. And now as parish priest he brought to bear on his work the same zeal and devotion to duty which distinguished him as curate and Chaplain to the Forces. To his instrumentality is due the present fine Catholic school, the last to be built by the Catholic authorities before the Education (Scotland) Act of 1918. From Duntocher Father Flynn was promoted to the old-established parish of St Mary's, Hamilton, where he was destined to pass the remaining sixteen years of his life. On the occasion of the celebration of the centenary of St Mary's, 1946, in recognition of his long and devoted service, he was promoted to the Chapter of the Archdiocese of Glasgow, by the Most Rev. Donald A. Campbell. On the division of the Archdiocese in 1948 he became an Honorary Canon of Glasgow, and was appointed a Consultor of the new Diocese of Motherwell. By this time, however, he was already broken in health, and the end came on the 25th February, 1949.

Of Canon Flynn the first thing that must be said is that he was a good and humble priest. True to the ideals set before him during his college years he was constant in prayer and meditation all his life. His ardent and simple devotion to Our Blessed Lady found expression in the many visits he paid to her shrine at Lourdes. In his pastoral work he was suspicious of 'new movements,' and rightly held that the maintenance of the strong and lively faith of our Catholic people must be based on the constant visitation of the priest to the homes, and on the constant teaching of religion by the clergy in the schools; and he himself, as long as his health permitted, was an example to those under him in these two respects. He would have little to do with 'Youth Movements' in the modern sense, and held that our Catholic Guilds should be independent of Education and Civil Authorities no matter how well-intentioned. In this his fears may or may not have been groundless, but his attitude showed how jealous he ever was of freedom and independence of action in all matters in which the Church was concerned.

His was a serious temperament, scrupulous to a degree, and exact in all that concerned the observance of canon and diocesan law; strict in discipline, but strictest always with himself. He was no respecter of persons, and what he had to say he said forcibly and with no beating about the bush. He was exact in affairs of business, and gave an attention to correspondence not always found among the clergy. He held in reverence the great names associated with the growth of the Church in Scotland, and he never tired of speaking of Archbishop Eyre and Archbishop Maguire who in his youth had ruled the Church in the West. He was not without a sense of humour, and at clerical gatherings he could keep things going with many a quip and many a witty riposte. But when all is said he will be remembered by the people among whom he laboured as the man of God and the faithful pastor of his flock.

The Right Reverend Monsignor Alexander Provost Hamilton (d. 1971)

Monsignor Hamilton was born in Glasgow on 19th June, 1887. He was educated at St Mungo's Academy, Blairs College,

Aberdeen, and at St Peter's College, Bearsden. He was ordained to the priesthood in June, 1914.

He was appointed as assistant priest to the church of Our Lady of Good Aid, Motherwell, until he joined the staff of St Peter's College to teach philosophy. The First War caused many students to enlist in the forces and the time came when the college was continued by the rector and two students. Monsignor Hamilton returned to pastoral work and served as an assistant at Holy Cross, Crosshill, until the end of the war. In the early days of 1919, students returned from the forces and were joined by students from Blairs College and colleges in Ireland. Monsignor Hamilton taught philosophy until after the departure of Monsignor Claeys in 1923. Moral theology then became his subject until he left the college to become parish priest of St Patrick's, Shieldmuir, Lanarkshire, in 1935. During his time in Shieldmuir the liturgy was carried out in full and the hall became the centre of the youth activities of the Diocese of Motherwell.

In 1949 Monsignor Hamilton was transferred to St Mary's, Hamilton, where he was destined to spend the remaining twenty-two years of his life. When the Cathedral Chapter of the Diocese of Motherwell was erected in the year 1952, he became one of its first canons, and on the death of Monsignor McGonagle he was elected as provost. Pope Pius XII named him as a Domestic Prelate in 1957.

In addition to the responsibilities consequent upon his official appointments as assistant priest, college professor or parish priest, Monsignor Hamilton always found time and enthusiasm for other activities which had far-reaching effects. He established a guild for the blind, which has brought wonderful help and consolation to many who are thus afflicted. Teachers and youth leaders delighted in his instructions on liturgy and church music. He was chaplain to the Guild of Catholic Nurses for many years. In the diocesan curia he was Officialis for some time. It could be said that Monsignor never refused to undertake any office or task which would be of value to the Church.

Perhaps details such as these might be applied in greater or less degree to other good priests who have gone to God to receive from His infinite bounty the promised reward of faithful service, but in the case of Monsignor Hamilton, his death would seem to mean something more. It marks the end of an era in the history of the Church in the west of Scotland . . . and it should not be allowed to pass into oblivion.

The name of Monsignor Alexander Hamilton must be forever linked with St Peter's College, Bearsden, which enshrined the spirit of that illustrious prelate, the Most Reverend Charles Eyre, first Archbishop of Glasgow in the restored hierarchy. He had been sent from Newcastle help solve the problem of division between the poor Highland crofters who had come to Glasgow to seek a better life and the Irish who had fled the famine in their homeland. The bitter differences which had arisen threatened the progress of the Church which was striving to emerge from the darkness of penal times. Gradually the factions were merged together and the Pugin churches which are still in our midst stand as witnesses to the united efforts of the Scottish and Irish Catholics of Glasgow.

St Peter's College, Bearsden, was founded and financed by Archbishop Eyre himself. There he gathered together his students for the priesthood, both Scottish and Irish. This was an important step towards healing the bitter divisions of the past. Herein lay the hopes of the archbishop that young men would be ordained from this college with one mind and one ambition, namely, the progress of the Church in the west of Scotland.

There came also a Continental influence from students who were German, Dutch, or Belgian. Amongst these one name stands out: the name of Octavius Francis Claeys. He came to Bearsden with all the cultural background of the great Seminary of Bruges. After a few years as assistant priest at St Agnes's, Lambhill, he came to the college staff, and it would be difficult to assess his influence on the college over many years. Apart from the fact that he was an able teacher in philosophy and theology, he exercised an influence in many fields of activity, both cultural and recreational. One of his most able students was Alexander Hamilton and it was no surprise when he returned to the college as a member of the staff. In these two professors the spirit of Archbishop Eyre was ever kept alive. War came to bring plans to a standstill but, when hostilities ceased in the year 1918, a new spirit pervaded the college and indeed the whole of the Church in Scotland. The reason could be found in the fact that, apart from the relief that came with peace returned to the world, an Act of Parliament took over our schools while retaining their Catholic character. This eased the burden of school and church debt in all parishes.

The effect was immediate. The Church seemed to come out into the light of day. During the early 1920s open-air processions gave expression to the joy that was in the hearts of the faithful. Carfin became a place of pilgrimage and in some measure its inspiration came from the college. Monsignor Hamilton was in the forefront of the Liturgical Revival and, with teachers and lay groups, he did much to teach Plain Song as the music of the Church par excellence.

The year 1925 was declared a Holy Year by Pope Pius XI. For the first time in their lives Catholic teachers were in the position of being able to consider the possibility of going to Rome. In the July of that year, under the leadership of the Most Reverend Donald Mackintosh, Archbishop of Glasgow, four hundred and fifty teachers set out to pay their respects and to offer allegiance to His Holiness, Pope Pius XI. Monsignor Hamilton had trained them in the singing of the mass. The archbishop celebrated Solemn High Mass at Notre Dame Cathedral in Paris on the way to Rome and the singing was truly wonderful. This was repeated in Rome in the church of San Silvestro. Again Monsignor Hamilton rendered the same service at the Beatification of Blessed John Ogilvie in 1929.

These occasions were but the outward expression of a faith that knew no doubts, and with leaders such as Monsignor Hamilton one would have thought that the Church could only go from strength to strength. Alas, a second war came, doubts have arisen, and all is not as well in the Church as the Church in the 1920s had augured. Monsignor adapted himself to the changes which came from the Church itself, but deplored the idea that nothing had been done in the past. It should be remembered that there was a time when most of our parishes could sing mass in Latin and join with the world in Rome or Lourdes in singing the Credo. Due to the wonderful efforts of Monsignor Hamilton there was a liturgical revival in this country before the vernacular was allowed.

In his latter days when he was unable to leave the presbytery, he welcomed old friends and delighted in the glories of the Church which are somewhat dimmed but should not be forgotten.

Very Rev. Hugh Canon Cahill, D.D. (d. 1990)

At the Funeral Mass in St Mary's Hamilton the following homily was given by Bishop Joseph Devine, Bishop of Motherwell:

Nearly thirty years ago, as a young priest half-way through a postgraduate course in Rome, I sat beside a man whom I had never met before, a man over 30 years my senior. We were an unlikely pairing that day, in late June of 1963, external examiners of the philosophy students in Cardross. The senior partner of the team was, of course, Canon Hugh. Then over 50, he must have seemed to me to be positively ancient, for that is how the eyes of the young perceive those who have crossed the barrier of the big 50. Clearer still is my memory of his text book approach, delivered laconically, even impersonally. I suppose he must have found my more flamboyant style puzzling. I know he did. He did not have to tell me. An arched eyebrow spoke volumes. He was entitled to the arch, for he had much more right to be in the examiner's chair than I at that point, in the light of who he was and what he had done.

Hugh Cahill was born on 13th July, a close shave there, 1905 in Rutherglen. A great gift from God was the family solidity of exemplary parents. Time and again, in that era, that was the background from which vocations sprang. It remains true to this day, despite the less obvious cohesion of family life. So, it was no great surprise to anyone to see Hugh Cahill take the first step towards the priesthood by leaving St Aloysius and entering Blairs College. A similar path was to be followed by his younger brother Thomas. Then it was off to Rome and the old Scots College in the city centre from which he was ordained to the priesthood for the Archdiocese of Glasgow, 28th February 1931. Successful final examinations in the summer of that year brought him his Doctorate in Divinity. On returning home a surprising turn of events overtook him. Due to temporary shortage in the Diocese of Dunkeld, his first appointment was to Sts Peter and Paul in the city of Dundee. He retained an affection for that city, quixotically always placing the emphasis on the first syllable in his pronunciation of the word. He remained there for 3 years. Then came a long sojourn of 17 years, perhaps best summarised in the phrase of dungeon, fire and sword. For he went to the Old College at Bearsden, fondly or perhaps not, referred to as the 'Den', right through the sword of war in 39-45, and beyond the fire of 1946. But he was not there except in a moral sense as a staff member of the college, for he was by then in Blairs again with the philosophy students. He returned to the unified St Peter's in the late 40s in its new setting at Darleith and Kilmahew in Cardross. Liberation came from the academic world to the pastoral life in 1951 as an assistant priest in St Brigid's, Baillieston, for a year. In 1952 he moved to Newmains as Parish Priest. Five years later he was to be found in All Saints, Coatdyke. At the end of 1961 he was transferred to New Stevenston and remained there for exactly a decade. I suspect that when he came here just over 18 years ago he would have known that this was to be his final appointment, becoming almost to the very day, this day, 18 years ago, a member of the Cathedral Chapter. He must have found it agreeable here. The old town, the old parish, the tradition and style of the community, all of these would have been to his taste. The walled garden and the semi-monastic appearance of the place must have given him the sense of permanence and solidity, like an image of the Church universal. But then came the turmoil of the late 60s and the upheavals, liturgically, theologically and morally, of the 70s. It was no longer his kind of era in terms of attitudes, no longer so familiar a church in terms of vision and outlook.

Apart from that brief encounter in the June of 1963, Canon Hugh Cahill was really only a name to me until I came to the Diocese in 1983. Quite soon that was to change substantially. Early in 1984 I came here to see him with a problem. The problem was that Fr. Alex Devanny, upon whom he had come to rely over the years and for whom he had a high regard, was due to become a parish priest. The Canon was very well aware of that fact. I raised with him the possibility that the most constructive solution would be that he should stay on here in retirement and Alex become the Parish Priest of St Mary's. The Canon could not have made it easier if he had tried. He looked at me for about 10 seconds and then said, 'Give me a pen and I'll sign on the dotted line'. The whole interview scarcely lasted a quarter of an hour.

Whatever else may have been the case, Canon Hugh Cahill always thought along straight lines. In that he was utterly consistent in life. For him grey areas were a kind of aberration. Reality was either black or white. He never found the mysteries of the truths of faith to be a problem, baffled by those of the Catholic community who did. What he did find troublesome was a rational problem which was reluctant to yield up its truth. Fr. Jim Foley gave me a splendid example of that in a recent chat he had with the Canon when he visited him in hospital a few weeks ago. The Canon told him that he had wrestled with a puzzle since 1930. And the problem? Could someone have formal certitude about something which was objectively erroneous? Well, he will have the answer now. Most people would not have bothered to inquire. Even more would not have understood the question.

I tell that story to illustrate the mind of a man troubled by the easy and quick assumptions, theological and moral, of a world which had lost or was losing its direction, a world defective in ethical consistency and increasingly detached from religious commitment. Such inconsistency and lack of commitment were completely foreign to Hugh Cahill. That is what leads me to the deep paradox which was his deeper truth. Publicly, in a pulpit, he was as different as could be imagined from the confessor in the confessional or the counsellor in the call room. It was as if there were two different people. In a pulpit he was forthright. In saying that, I somewhat understate the case. But in the arena of the one to one, his was a great apostolate. He knew human weakness and fallibility, not least from his own reflections upon himself. Those who encountered him in that private arena were much graced and much blessed.

I have scarcely done justice to a long life lived against the backdrop of two world wars, the depression of the 20s and 30s, the slow recovery of the 50s. But much the greater part of the Canon's life, in his formation and priestly ministry was in an era of the greatest stability which the Church had known here since the Reformation. It was that experience of internal stability which gave the Canon a delight in order, an ordered mind, an ordered community, an ordered Church. But the whole history of the Church shows us a different picture, turmoil to peace, weakness to greatness, dying to rise again. Each of us has to endure that pattern of dying to rise again, every day, and then at the last, as did Jesus before us. That has been the whole thrust of our readings today. To the best of his ability he sought to be the Lord's dutiful servant. To the best of ours we commend him to the Lord of all, the all merciful Father. AMEN.

Parish Structures and Activities in the 1990s

The following extracts from the parish handbook give an indication of the nature of St Mary's in the 1990s. There are obvious similarities with the past, notably in the range of organisations devoted to social and community activities. The most remarkable difference, however, is in the transformation of the role of the laity. In this parish, lay members run the office, act as eucharistic ministers, raise significant sums for church building and renovation purposes and organise children's masses. The impact of Vatican 2, the shortage of priests and the new aspirations of a well-educated Catholic community are all factors in this. Nevertheless, the parish priest still maintains the role of spiritual leader while trying to guide the energies of his flock.

St Mary's Mission Statement

1. To build up a prayerful community with a rich sacramental life.
2. To reach out in particular to the young people of the parish and to serve their needs.
3. To reach out to our fellow Christians and others and to learn from them.
4. To work together, priest and people, in a spirit of shared responsibility, efficiently and co-operatively.
5. To welcome others into that community, through warmth, instruction, and celebration.

Pastoral Renewal Team

This group was set up in November 1992 to plan, initiate, and evaluate the points stated in the parish mission statement.

The parish mission statement has five points and the team has been most active in an attempt to establish a parish office as a means of improving the working of the parish.

The office has now opened and members of the parish are encouraged to use it either to make contact (e.g. newcomers) or to obtain information. This becomes all the more necessary in view of the fact that Monsignor Devanny presently has diocesan responsibility for the priests in the area.

Church Office

FUNCTIONS

Organising Mgr. Devanny's business dairy. Anyone wishing to see Mgr. Devanny should make an appointment.

Dealing with incoming and outgoing mail.

Taking bookings for weddings, christenings, etc.

Dealing with requests for Mass cards, baptismal certificates etc.

Compiling a register of new parishioners.

Collating information about parishioners in hospital or housebound.

Production of weekly newsletter.

Liaison with diocesan office.

Liaison with St Mary's primary school.

Parish Bus

Each Sunday there is a bus which tours the parish to allow those in the slightly less central areas to get to 11.30 Mass. It starts at Dalziel Street at approximately 11.00 a.m., goes up Auchencampbell Street thence to Portland Park, stops at Gateside Street and then to the Church.

Eucharistic Ministers

The first five ministers of the Eucharist in St Mary's were commissioned on Holy Thursday 1985. Over the years that number has grown until at the present moment there are eighteen ministers operating within the parish.

Their main function was initially to assist in the distribution of communion at Sunday mass and on holidays of obligation. More recently they have been entrusted with the duty of taking the Holy Eucharist to the housebound people in the parish. A rota system operates in order that the Eucharist is taken regularly to those who are unable to come to church.

The group is now trying to establish an equally regular service to the various nursing homes in the parish.

The Parish Group

The Parish Group was the first organisation Mgr. Devanny started when he joined the parish some fourteen years ago. The group was formed to co-ordinate the activities of the parish.

It began by organising social functions in the church hall which were needed to raise money to bring the hall up to a reasonable standard. It also started the 200 Club to raise funds. Several thousand pounds have been spent to bring it up to its present condition.

The Friends of St Mary's

The Friends of St Mary's were formed to help raise money to finance the refurbishment of the Church building and its surrounding area.

The main way this has been done is by organising a lottery. This has been very successful and has now entered its sixth year.

The main refurbishment programme is now complete but there are many more improvements which will be made in the future and funds will need to be raised for this and to pay off our debts.

Third World Group

St Mary's Third World Group was formed in March 1985 in the wake of the terrible television reports of the famine in Ethiopia. During the last nine years it has had many varied fund-raising events, including jumble sales, book sales, Burns suppers, art shows, cabaret nights, 24-hour fasts, sponsored runs in Strathclyde Park, sponsored cycles round Millport, carol singing in Hamilton town centre (now an annual event), fashion shows, and dinner dances. It is also involved in the education side of the problems of the Third World, and as well as raising money we try to raise awareness of the many injustices suffered by Third World countries – the outstanding debt, unfair trading, poor education, etc.

The Group has welcomed many speakers over the years including SCIAF staff and field workers who have been to Brazil and Nicaragua, a nun who worked in Africa and Bishop Mone, the president of SCIAF, celebrated mass in St Mary's and gave a talk and slide show in the hall afterwards.

The Third World Group organise SCIAF Sunday decorating the church and giving a small talk on SCIAF work and aims at all masses. The group is now responsible for St Mary's representation on the Hamilton Branch of Christian Aid and organise St Mary's participation in all Christian Aid events, especially Christian Aid Week.

To date more than £100,000 has been raised, all of which has been used for famine relief and development in the Third World. All of this has been possible only due to the generosity of the parishioners of St Mary's and to the many Hamilton businesses and shopkeepers who have supported events.

St Vincent de Paul Society

A conference of the Society was established in St Mary's in 1853. This year is the 141st anniversary of service in the Parish. In addition to visiting the sick and elderly in the Parish, visitations are also carried out by members of the conference to hospitals, residential homes, and prisons. Help in cash or kind is provided to the needy and a furniture project at diocesan level is supported. As part of the Society's work in the third world St Mary's Hamilton is twinned with St Mary's Koothrappally, Kerela State, India. For the past thirty-two years, through the generosity of parishioners and St Mary's Third World Group, it has been possible to provide considerable financial assistance to the twin conference. The projects assisted include house building and the provision of sewing machines and other material objects to enable poor families to earn a living.

The Catholic Men's Society

The St Mary's branch of the Catholic Men's Society has been re-established recently. At present it meets on the second Monday of each month. The aim of the Society is to help men to learn more about their Faith. This is done by planned discussion in a fairly informal atmosphere.

Children's Liturgy Group

This is a group of about fifteen parents who meet monthly to prepare the liturgy for the children's Sunday 10.00 a.m. mass.

On Sundays, the children are divided into two groups, pre- and post- Holy Communion groups, and are provided with a liturgy to suit their age groups.

Special feasts, e.g. Christmas and Easter, are usually given special emphasis and the liturgy is portrayed in a play or mime.

The group is supported by the Parish and also runs an annual coffee morning to cover the cost of crayons, carts etc.

Annually the Liturgy Group:

a. holds a parish reception for the First Holy Communicants.
b. runs a summer or Christmas party/outing
c. collects Christmas gifts for needy children of Hamilton

d. collects Easter eggs for needy children of Hamilton
e. holds an Easter Bazaar to raise money for SCIAF

Social Concerns Group

The Social Concerns Group sprang from the Parish of St Mary's participation in the diocesan Renew programme some years ago.

At first parishioners were invited to express an interest in becoming members of the group whose main target was visitation and support of elderly/disabled people who were members of the Parish.

The initial task of the group was to make contact with a list of parishioners given by the Parish Priest who seemed to require some contact from the Parish. The objective at that point in time was to create a mechanism whereby the Parish through the visitor was able to maintain a tangible link with mainly housebound people enabling them to feel part of the Parish, be informed about developments within the Parish and receive any help necessary to enable them to deal with personal problems brought about by their personal situation.

At an early stage it was recognised that although this contact was in itself valuable from a given point of view it might be further enhanced at a more spiritual level by having the visitor also act as a Eucharistic minister. Some development has taken place on this front in so far as several members of the group are currently Eucharistic ministers although the two roles are not yet formally aligned.

The next stage in growth of the group was to design referral forms and inform parishioners both of the existence of the group and the means of making contact. These documents were made available at the rear of the church but to date over a year later no referral had been received by the Social Concerns Group.

St Mary's Music Group

St Mary's Music Group was formed five years ago, having been started just before Christmas 1989 by Eddie Bradshaw (R.I.P.).

The group consists of children and young people of the Parish who play at the children's 10 o'clock mass every Sunday and at other children's services throughout the year, including the Third World Group's annual carol service in the town centre.

Stepping Stones Playgroup

The Stepping Stones Playgroup meets in the church hall on Tuesday and Thursday mornings. The group runs from 9.30 a.m. to 11.00 a.m. and caters for children from 3 to 5 years of age.

ST. MARY'S. HAMILTON

Concert

and Presentation of Testimonial

to

The Rev. Thomas J. Winning, D.C.L.

GRANADA THEATRE. HAMILTON
SUNDAY. 20th OCTOBER. 1957
at 7.30 p.m.

The Right Rev. Mgr. A. Canon Hamilton. P.P., V.F
Presiding

SOUVENIR PROGRAMME

R W DICK PRINTER HAMILTON

The souvenir programme for presentation to a young curate of St Mary's, the future Cardinal Thomas J. Winning.